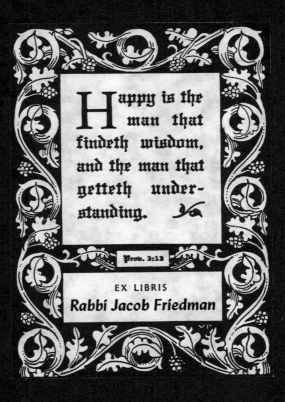

SEVENTY FACETS

SEVENTY FACETS

A COMMENTARY
ON THE
TORAH

FROM THE PAGES OF

GERSHOM GORENBERG

JASON ARONSON INC.
Northvale, New Jersey
London

This book was set in 12 pt. Antiqua by Alpha Graphics of Pittsfield, N.H.

10 9 8 7 6 5 4 3 2 1

Library of Congress Cataloging-in-Publication Data

Seventy facets: a commentary on the Torah/from the pages of the
   Jerusalem report; edited by Gershom Gorenberg.
     p.   cm.
   Includes index.
   ISBN 1-56821-904-0 (alk. paper)
     1. Bible. O.T. Pentateuch-Commentaries.   I. Gorenberg,
Gershom.   II. Jerusalem report.
BS1225.3.S268 1996
222'.107—dc20   96-14581
                                                           CIP

Manufactured in the United States of America. Jason Aronson Inc. offers books and cassettes. For information and catalog write to Jason Aronson Inc., 230 Livingston Street, Northvale, New Jersey 07647.

In memory

of

Marcia Kretzmer

CONTENTS

EXODUS

SPECIAL READINGS

HOLIDAYS

INTRODUCTION

Gershom Gorenberg

"The Torah has seventy faces," says the midrash in
Bemidbar Rabbah. That is, it has manifold meanings;
no single understanding can contain its fullness. The
statement comes as part of an allegorical interpretation of the "one bowl weighing seventy shekels" (Numbers 7) that the head of each tribe donated to the Tabernacle in the desert. And the midrash continues:
"Why does it say 'one bowl'? This symbolizes the
Torah, which must be one, as is said (Numbers 15:16):
'You will have one Torah and one law. . . .'" The seventy
faces are seventy facets of a single gem; even if no
human eye can take in all of them at once, they remain
parts of a whole.

The idea of diversity is taken even further in *Shmot
Rabbah*. Commenting on Exodus 20:15, "And all the
people saw the voices" when God spoke at Sinai, the
midrash says: "The text does not say 'voice,' but rather
'voices' . . . The voice went out to every Israelite according to his ability: the elders according to their ability,

the young men according to theirs . . . the women according to theirs, and also to Moses according to his ability." Or as the sixteenth-century kabbalistic master Rabbi Yitzhak Luria said, "There are 600,000 aspects and meanings in the Torah," one for each of the Israelites who left Egypt and stood at Sinai.

The Torah's unity and diversity can be seen graphically in its two traditional formats. The scroll read in the synagogue presents only the text itself, ceremonially stark and solemn, without even vowel markings or punctuation. But in the *beit midrash*, the study hall, students use *mikra'ot gedolot*, the "expanded scripture." Open it, and you'll find the text of the Torah surrounded by arguing Jews. In the edition I use, for instance, there are three separate Aramaic translations, six medieval commentaries, and two commentaries on commentaries. In his exegesis, Rabbi Avraham Ibn Ezra cites sundry other scholars, often to rip them to shreds. Ramban—Rabbi Moshe ben Nahman—regularly quotes Ibn Ezra, sometimes agreeing with him, often quarreling. In place of solemnity come irony and intellectual ripostes. You can see the voices.

Then again, there are limits to the debate on those pages. Ibn Ezra, the most daring polemicist, quotes Karaite scholars, and on rare occasions even agrees with one. He also hints, most guardedly, that several verses in the Torah were added after Moses' time. But the commentaries we find in *mikra'ot gedolot* all accept that the Torah was given at Sinai, that it must be understood through the Oral Torah of rabbinic tradition, and that it contains 613 commandments eternally incumbent upon all Jews.

In our day, such agreement on basic principles is gone; the Jewish debate has become far more diverse. Where some see the Torah as a single Mosaic text, others find a mosaic of historical documents. Some read the Bible as national literature rather than religious scripture. Rabbis of different denominations take differing views of how binding the commandments are and how they should be interpreted. Feminists seek the voices of biblical women. What remains, creating unity, is that the debate is about one text.

It was this recognition of a people united by debate about the Book that guided Marcia Kretzmer when she created *The Jerusalem Report*'s column on the weekly Torah portion in 1991. She believed that a Jewish magazine published in Jerusalem must create a place for discussion of the Torah. Equally, she believed that an independent magazine that covers and is read by the Jewish world could not restrict itself to the voice of a single rabbi or scholar, no matter how prominent. It would provide the debate; it would allow its reader to "see the voices." The only position that *The Jerusalem Report* would take was that Jews can be brought together by studying—and disagreeing about—Torah.

Accordingly, she invited a wide range of prominent rabbis, academic Bible scholars, writers, and poets to contribute—from Israel and the Diaspora; Orthodox, Conservative, Reform, and secular; women and men; rabbis of settlements in the territories and proponents of territorial compromise. Since taking over as editor of "The People and the Book" in 1992, I have sought to fulfill Marcia Kretzmer's original vision. A number of writers, reflecting divergent views, have become regular contributors, but I have also continued seeking out new voices. Recognizing the diversity among our readers, I have asked all writers to try to speak both to those with extensive knowledge of the Torah and to those who have less Jewish background but share curiosity and intellectual sophistication. To my delight, the contributors take very different approaches to the text; often I disagree with their conclusions.

For this book, I have selected seventy articles—one on each of the fifty-four weekly Torah portions, along with articles on the four special readings of the spring and on the holidays. (In the case of the holidays, some essays deal with the readings for the days, others with the day itself and its meaning.) Choosing was not easy; I was forced to leave out many excellent and provocative pieces of writing. In particular, I made the difficult decision to leave out some fine poetry that has appeared in "The People and the Book."

I have, however, striven to retain the column's eclecticism, to ensure that the book shows seventy facets of Torah. In some cases, the debate is explicit. In writing on *Tazria*, Tzvi Marx considers how the Torah can be read to accept homosexuality—and disagrees with the approach taken by his Orthodox colleague, Moshe Tendler, in his comments on Rosh Hashanah. Discussing *Hukkat*, Reuven Hammer criticizes the position taken by Yeshayahu Leibowitz in his commentary on *Shmini* that a person who "intends to worship God, but derives satisfaction for himself from this worship . . . is [offering] illicit fire."

Elsewhere, the differences in philosophy are present even if not stated. Blu Greenberg, writing on *Dvarim*, states that "Observance of the law . . . becomes a measure of integrity in the covenantal relationship" between God and Israel as laid out in Deuteronomy. Commenting on *Ekev*, Mark Silverman calls precisely that convenantal relationship into question, asking how the people of Israel could "escape being incapacitated by guilt at their inability to live up to the expectations of their relentlessly demanding and oft-outraged father?" Likewise, commentaries grow out of varied ways of reading: Reform rabbi and scholar W. Gunther Plaut uncovers the Torah's historical context in the portions of *Vayekhi* and *Tzav*; poet Susan Afterman turns regularly to kabbalistic and hasidic understandings; Hillel Halkin brings a literary critic's eye to the text.

A few of these articles sparked angry letters from readers when they appeared in *The Jerusalem Report*. They appear here nonetheless. It would be surprising if any reader could agree with every one of the seventy essays; that is not the book's goal. Rather, it is to portray the range of debate among Jews today about the Torah. I hope that it will also perform the functions of the traditional study in *hevruta*, in which two students read together, contending with each other's views: to provoke, to cause questions, to demand thought and rereading of the text.

I am grateful to all those who have contributed to "The People and the Book," including those whose essays or poetry, unfortunately, could not appear here. I have been spiritually and intellectually enriched by working with them. I also thank Ronnie Hope and my other colleagues at *The Jerusalem Report* who have taken part in the editing process; Rochelle Furstenberg, who participated in the original discussions that gave "The People and the Book" its character; and Ruth Frank, who made publishing this book possible.

In particular, I am grateful to two people who are no longer with us. Professor Yeshayahu Leibowitz, a courageous man of faith, honored us with his contributions; he died in 1994 in the great fullness of his days and work. Marcia Kretzmer, a woman truly described by the words "The Torah of loving-kindness is on her lips" (Proverbs 31:26), passed away before her time. This book is a tribute to her memory.

GENESIS

A PLAN FOR LIFE

Breshit: Genesis 1:1–6:8

Irving Greenberg

Genesis is not so much an account of creation as a statement of God's plan. It answers the question: What kind of world did God intend to create? *Breshit* describes the world as it will be when God and humanity finish their work. Subsequently in the Bible, we learn that in the process of perfecting the world, Jews will lead the way, teaching, setting an example, working alongside others, serving as witness to God's purpose and as "a light unto the nations."

What then is the true—Divine—pattern of the world? The Torah's threefold answer cuts through a welter of conflicting evidence and surface contradictions:

- This world is moving from chaos to order. In the beginning there was chaos and void (the Big Bang?); now there is natural law and order.
- Contrary to the commonsense perception that death ultimately wins out—for all living things die—the Torah teaches that the world is moving

3

from non-life to life. The universe is created by an infinite source of life, and by Divine will, life emerges, reproduces, proliferates, and expands. God intends the world to be filled with life—especially in its highest form, humanity. Therefore, God blesses living creatures and calls upon them to "be fruitful and multiply."

To emphasize this, God repeats this commandment/blessing to humanity. According to the Talmud, that means parents are obligated to have two children. But it then cites Isaiah's view of the creation story: "The world was created not to be empty but to be settled." So the rabbis add an obligation to go further: Only if two parents have three or more children will the surplus of life over death grow.

· Life is moving in a direction: becoming more like God. In Genesis, God displays infinite capacities for life, freedom, power, consciousness, and relationship. These are the qualities that life, created by God, possesses. In human beings, these qualities reach their highest development. The human being—man and woman—is created "in the image of God."

This is the source of humanity's mission. Because human beings are Godlike, God calls them into partnership—to rule this world and shape it. To this end, humans are given control over the earth and over other forms of life as well. But as the Torah makes clear, the human is "to work and guard it." The human must not abuse the world or kill. Since God wants life to win out, ideally all living creatures—including human beings—should be vegetarians. "And to all the animals on land, to all the birds of the sky, and to everything that creeps on earth, in which there is the breath of life, [I give] all the green plants for food" (Genesis 1:30). No life should exist by killing other life.

In sum, Genesis begins by teaching that God's vision and purpose is a world in which we shall see the triumph of life. Quantitatively, the world must be filled with life. Qualitatively, life must be sustained properly. Humans, in particular, must be treated reverently, for they are in the image of God. So in God's plan, there is ultimately no room for poverty or hunger, for war or oppression, for sickness or death. In Isaiah's words: "They shall beat their swords into plowshares . . . They shall not learn war anymore"; "They shall neither do evil nor destroy . . . for the earth is full of knowledge of the Lord"; "Death will be swallowed up in eternity."

Eons have passed since creation began and humanity made its appearance. Yet, the vision of *tikkun olam* (perfection) retains its force. Almost four thousand years have passed since the first Jew lived on earth, but the vision of Genesis remains central to the Jewish mission. As Rabbi Joseph Soloveitchik wrote in *Halakhic Man*: "The dream of creation is the central idea in the halakhic consciousness—the idea of the importance of man as a partner of the Almighty in the act of creation. . . . Man's task is to . . . transform the emptiness in being into a perfect and holy existence. . . ."

SECOND CHANCE

Noah: Genesis 6:9–11:32

Immanuel Jakobovits

Perhaps there is no section in the Torah that raises a more profound problem than this portion. The destruction in the Flood of virtually the whole of humanity challenges more than God's justice. It raises questions concerning the whole design of the Creator in bringing the universe into existence. Was it an admission of failure, on a scale never repeated in history?

The text itself seems to invite such a suggestion, daring as it is. "And the Lord repented [*vayinnahem*] that He had made man on the earth and it grieved Him in His heart" (Genesis 6:6). There is no hint here that *man* frustrated the Divine design.

Our Sages made the same point, in an even bolder fashion, in their interpretation of the sacrifice to be made to each New Moon, referred to in the Torah as a "sin-offering *unto the Lord*" (Numbers 28:15). There are other sacrifices known as sin-offerings, but no other one is described as being "unto the Lord." The Sages explained this, as Rashi phrased it in his commentary,

7

as an invitation by God to "seek atonement for *Me* for having reduced the moon." The reference is to the allegorical rabbinic story that the sun and the moon were originally created as equally "great luminaries" (Genesis 1:16); when the moon protested against the reign of two suns, it was made smaller, into a "little luminary." The plain text suggests that the Creator sought atonement through Israel for the initial mistake in the creation plans (involving two suns instead of one), which thus required correction.

What a staggering thought! Every New Moon we are to be reminded that something went wrong in the plan of creation. Even the physical world was at first defective. So the story of creation begins with a fault that required correction and it ends with the world's all-but-complete annihilation in the Flood.

The message is awesome. Even God, so to speak, could not or did not make a perfect world on the first try. There could be no greater comfort to man than the knowledge that even He had to start a second time.

The very name Noah is explained in the Torah as meaning "this one shall *comfort* us [*yenahamenu*] in our work." "And he repented [*vayinnahem*] that he had made man on the earth . . ." quoted above, derives from the same root.

Man could never be creative if he could not afford to fail the first time and then to start all over again. The ability to make mistakes renders history possible. The very definition of progress is to move from a less perfect state to a better one.

No epoch has testified more dramatically than ours to the enormity of human error being superseded by a new and more successful effort. The sequel to the Nazi evil was the rebirth of the Jewish state, and the self-destruction of Communism will generate a renaissance of moral and spiritual values, if only in terms of human rights and of national freedom.

This, the story of Noah tells us, is the way which man shall be comforted: In the capacity to atone for error and to begin afresh in his spiritual evolution toward the ultimate goal of human brotherhood and the fulfilling moral norms set down for all mankind through God's commandments to Noah after the Flood.

An Ancestral Fragrance

Lekh Lekha: Genesis 12:1–17:27

Stuart Schoffman

At the age of 75, Abraham the idol-smasher finally leaves his father's house in Haran—Terah, that cranky Mesopotamian, is 145 and hale enough to live another 60 years—and makes for Canaan: a new life, a glorious destiny, an everlasting covenant. At age 86, he sires his first child, Ishmael. At 99, the patriarch performs the tricky feat of auto-circumcision—with the Almighty, according to a legend cited by Rashi, lending His Divine hand to help steady the knife.

Thus Abraham teaches us that you're never too old to make radical changes.

The Talmud, in Tractate *Rosh Hashanah*, lists five things that are capable of canceling the harsh decrees of heaven. These are almsgiving, prayer, and penitence, of course; but also changing one's name, and one's address. Abraham's wife Sarah, says the Talmud, changed her name from Sarai, and thereafter ceased to be infertile—bearing (at age 90) Abraham's younger but preferred son Isaac. As for changing location, noted the rabbis, it is written (Genesis 12:1), "The Lord said to Abram, 'Go forth from your native land,'" and then, in the very next breath, "'I will make of you a great nation.'"

If Abraham and Sarah were the first Jews to make *aliyah*, they set a pattern of revolutionary behavior that would be emulated by their progeny four thousand years later. Multitudes of bold Zionist pioneers left their parents' homes in the Diaspora, changed their names—from Gruen to Ben-Gurion, Myerson to Meir—and reclaimed the land promised by God to Abraham and his offspring.

Some of these offspring continue to take literally the boundaries of the Promised Land indicated in Genesis 15:18—"from the river of Egypt to the great river, the river Euphrates"—but most prefer to take a lesson from Abraham's Solomonic settling of a territorial dispute with his nephew Lot (Genesis 13:8–9): "Let there be no strife between you and me . . . for we are kinsmen. Is not the whole land before you? Let us separate: If you go north, I will go south, and if you go south, I will go north." No sooner did Abraham receive the land from God, than he was already changing its contours, giving a chunk away to avoid conflict.

Curiouser still, at the first sign of trouble—a famine in Canaan, barely five verses after Abraham arrives there from Haran—the father of the Jewish people is out the door and down in bountiful Egypt (Genesis 12:10–20).

As the Israeli novelist A.B. Yehoshua observed in his trenchant essay "Exile as a Neurotic Solution": "It transpires that the first *oleh* [immigrant to Israel] was also the first *yored* [emigrant from Israel]. . . . It is strange to think that this man, who gave up so much in leaving his father's house, having finally reached the Promised Land, could leave it so easily and choose to go into exile."

Perhaps Abraham is showing us that without exile, there is no redemption. Kabbalists in sixteenth-century Safed argued that Abraham's sudden trip to Egypt—where Sarah, pretending to be Abraham's sister, is sprung from Pharaoh's palace after God afflicts the Egyptians with "mighty plagues"—signifies that one cannot reach perfection unless he has descended into evil and risen from it. But maybe it's simply that Jews, paradoxically, need to wander, no less than they need a home.

Abraham, says the midrash in *Breshit Rabbah*, is likened to a vial of perfume, whose fragrance is wafted only when it is carried about, not when it is stoppered and left in a corner. "Thus the Lord said to Abraham: 'Take yourself from place to place, and your name will become great in the world.'" Or as the Yiddish humorist Mendele Mocher Seforim wrote: "As soon as father Abraham conceives of Judaism, the process of *lekh lekha*—get moving—begins."

Nothing, it would seem, is unchangeable—nothing except the covenant, the *brit*, carved as it is into the flesh of Abraham's descendants, blood relative and convert alike. And yet, is not mutability the very essence of the *brit*? The story is told of Rabbi Akiba, who was asked by a Roman nobleman why, if foreskins are made to be removed, males are born uncircumcised. "Man," replied the rabbi, "is required to improve upon nature."

And, one might add, upon human nature. If God's extravagant promises to Abraham tempt us—and how can they not?—into complacency and chauvinism, may the patriarch's restlessness and iconoclasm yank us, generation after generation, back onto the righteous road.

THE BODILY SIGN

Vayera: Genesis 18:1–22:24

Daniel Landes

> *And when his son Isaac was eight days old,*
> *Avraham circumcised him, as God had*
> *commanded him.*
> —Genesis 21:4

Circumcision has always been a scandal in Western civilization. The ancient Greeks opposed this marring of the body. Performing nude in the gymnasium, one displayed the achievements of a perfect soul within an unmutilated and thus perfect body. The Greeks viewed *brit milah* as an affront to nature and saw the circumcised phallus as parochially barring Jewish men from having intercourse with non-Jewish women. For the Greeks, *brit milah* was at once unnatural and racist.

Christianity, with its decision to win converts, dispensed with the "burden" of ritual circumcision as an obstacle to spiritual marketing. Circumcision of the flesh, which symbolized acceptance of the whole Law, was to be replaced by circumcision of the heart—that

15

is, faith alone. Dispirited by these attacks, Jews on the margins throughout history gave up on *brit milah* and even performed the dangerous practice of epispasm to hide the "blemish" of circumcision. In our day, circumcision has become the target of a three-pronged attack within the Jewish community itself.

The most common angle of attack is to view *brit milah* as a surgical procedure—and then find it wanting. The benefits of reduced cancers in Jewish males and their sexual partners, critics argue, can be achieved more easily through common cleanliness. Whatever the gains, they say, the baby's pain is too high a cost—though, in fact, a newborn's neural connections are not well-developed and the pain is minimal. Some argue that if circumcision is performed, anaesthesia must be used—though anaesthesia itself creates serious health risks. Others argue that only doctors should be allowed to circumcise. Circumcision, they argue, is "an unnecessary medical practice" that only mars the body, and should be eliminated or tightly controlled.

The second angle of attack is to see *brit milah* as did Reform Judaism's founder, Abraham Geiger: as "a barbaric bloody act, which fills the father with anxiety and puts the new mother into a state of morbid tension." Could it not be replaced, followers of this approach ask, with a form of "spiritual" initiation into religion, as in Christianity? In this view, *brit milah* mars the body without elevating the soul.

In addition, the old canard of *brit milah* as mutilation has begun to emanate in a new form from feminist circles. It goes: Jewish men have severe problems relating to women. The problems go back to the beginning of their identity formation, when ritual circumcision—a symbolic, brutal near-castration—is performed by their fathers or surrogates. The eventual result is sexual rage and frustration, which Jewish men express through abuse of women. For this group, *brit milah* mars the soul through the marring of the body.

The best response remains Maimonides' analysis in his *Guide for the Perplexed*. Maimonides was a physician, but the case he makes for circumcision is not medical, but spiritual, communal, and moral. *Brit milah*, he says, is a "bodily sign" demonstrating membership in the community that proclaims the unity of God. As such, it is a mark of spiritual distinction. On the communal level, the bodily mark encourages "mutual love" between "those who all bear the same sign, which forms for them a sort of covenant." *Brit milah* is therefore not just one of the 613 commandments. It remains the core sign of male Jewish identity, reminding Jewish men to save their sexual charms for covenantal partners only, namely, their Jewish wives.

Provocatively, what Maimonides offers as "strongest of the reasons for circumcision" has a feminist ring: that men have a tendency to mistreat women because of their need for sexual gratification. Circumcision "has not been prescribed with a view to perfect what is defective congenitally (i.e., the glans) but to perfect what is defective morally." *Brit milah* is meant to signify the ability to limit (not eliminate!) the demands of sexual excitement in order to promote self-control, concern for the other, and a moral vision within the full expression of passion. It is the ultimate symbol of the Jewish love for life built upon restraint and sacrifice.

THE ONES CUT OFF

Hayyei Sarah: Genesis 23:1–25:18

David Curzon

Today when I read in the portion of *Hayyei Sarah* of
Abraham's purchase of the cave at Makhpelah, the
massacre at that site in February 1994 intrudes on my
thoughts. Its intrusion forces me to see the theme of
reconciliation that exists in the Jewish tradition concerning *Hayyei Sarah*. In the text itself we have Abraham bowing to the Hittites and describing himself as
a stranger among them who wants to purchase a permanent claim to a small part of their land. Abraham
is portrayed as willing to ignore the advantage taken
of him by the seller in order to have the privilege of
owning some of this land.

Later in the Torah portion, at Genesis 25:1, we are told
that at the end of his life "Abraham took another wife,
and her name was Keturah." In the midrash of *Breshit
Rabbah* we find the flat assertion, attributed to Rabbi
Yehudah, that Keturah was none other than Hagar. This
midrash implies that Abraham kept in touch with Hagar
and Ishmael after he expelled them from his home,

which was also their home. As the late Yeshayahu Leibowitz commented, in remarks on Israel's Army Radio:
"We can see from the midrash and *Aggadah* to what
extent this incident bothered pious Torah scholars." In
the midrash's version of events, Abraham must have
made secret trips to see Hagar and Ishmael during the
intervening years before he married Hagar, like the
secret meetings held over many years between Israeli
prime ministers and King Hussein.

At the portion's end, after Abraham's death, there is
the surprising reappearance of Ishmael, apparently
mourning his father Abraham in harmony with his
estranged brother Isaac: "And Isaac and Ishmael his
sons buried him in the cave of Makhpelah" (Genesis
25:9).

My eye is also caught by a midrash on Abraham, also
in *Breshit Rabbah,* in which the anonymous *darshan,*
or exegete, quotes the first phrase of the first psalm,
"Happy is the man," comments "This is Abraham," and
then shows, phrase by phrase, the application of the
psalm to Abraham's life. The texts the *darshan* uses
to prove his assertion are, of course, drawn from the
Torah. In the spirit of reconciliation, I will follow this
midrash, using verses on Abraham from the Koran as
my prooftexts:

> *Happy is the man:* This is Abraham, as it is said in the Koran,
> Sura 4, "And God took Abraham for a friend."
>
> *that walks not in the counsel of the wicked,* as it is said in
> the Koran, Sura 21, with God speaking in the royal plural,
> "We gave Abraham his rectitude."
>
> *nor sat in the seat of the scornful,* as it is said in the Koran,
> Sura 11, "Our messengers came to Abraham with good tid-
> ings; they said, 'Peace!'"
>
> *He shall be like a tree planted by streams of water, that brings
> forth fruit in its season,* as it is said in the Koran, Sura 2,
> "Abraham said, 'My Lord, make this land secure and pro-
> vide its people with fruits.'"

and in whatever he does, he shall prosper, as it is said in the Koran, Sura 21, referring to the midrashic story of Abraham being cast into the fiery furnace by Nimrod, "We said, 'O fire, be coolness and safety for Abraham.'"

For the Lord regards the way of the righteous, but the way of the wicked shall perish, as it is said in the Koran, Sura 108, "Surely those who hate are the ones cut off."

This dictum, "Those who hate are the ones cut off," is both a psychological truth of the inner life of the individual and a political policy essential for peace. As it was said by Prime Minister Yitzhak Rabin, speaking of Baruch Goldstein, the murderer of the Cave of Makhpelah, and as we rightly require the leaders of the children of Ishmael to say about each of their terrorists and murderers: You are not part of us.

In the name of the collaborative effort needed to maintain peace, as it is said at the close of *Hayyei Sarah*: "And Isaac and Ishmael his sons buried Abraham in the cave of Makhpelah."

SEE NO EVIL

Toldot: Genesis 25:19–28:9

Baruch Feldstern

Isaac could not see. Although Genesis 27:1 may record this more delicately—"When Isaac grew old, his eyes were too dim to see"—no euphemism can obscure the stark fact that he was blind.

This is nothing to be ashamed of unless, of course, physical defects signal underlying character weaknesses. Strict rationalists, like Rashi's grandson, Rabbi Shmuel ben Meir (Rashbam), are inclined to dismiss such a view ("from old age," he comments on Isaac's blindness, citing a biblical parallel and relying, after all, on the explicit statement quoted above). Modern counterparts of these commentators point out that the ophthalmic observation is simply a bit of foreshadowing, necessary if we are to understand how Jacob could deceive his father with a goat's-hair sweater and make off with brother Esau's blessing.

But the straightforward simplicity of these explanations shouldn't make us lose sight of biblical hints that point in a different direction. After all, Moses' un-

diminished eyesight is considered sufficiently note-
worthy to be recorded in his death notice (Deuteronomy 34:7), a curious item in the obituary of our greatest prophet unless it reflects significance beyond the
merely physical. Moreover, an interesting pattern
of moral linkage does emerge if we look (as do the
rabbis, for example, in Midrash *Shmuel* 8:8) for a common denominator among the few blind characters in
the Bible and see that it lies in the shortcomings of
their protégés: Eli, the high priest whose greedy, las-
civious sons desecrated their priestly office; Ahijah
the Shilonite, the prophetic patron behind Jereboam's
idolatrous revolt against Solomon (1 Kings 11); and
Isaac.

The rabbis view Isaac's blindness as a kind of moral
myopia, reflected in his astonishing lack of awareness
that Jacob, not Esau, was his proper heir. This lapse was
magnified in rabbinic eyes, which saw Esau as a vir-
tual devil who not only preferred soup to birthright
and Hittite women to virtuous cousins, but also raped,
plundered, worshiped idols, and murdered—not acci-
dentally the crimes of the Roman oppressor in rabbinic
times, for which "Esau" served as a politically safe
alias. However, our interest in the causes of Isaac's
blindness and in the variety of rabbinic diagnoses need
not depend on a desire to follow the biblical plot or a
concern with the politics of Roman Palestine. As envi-
sioned by the rabbis, Isaac's blindness becomes a metaphor through which we can consider why good people
overlook evil staring them in the face.

Sometimes we think it pays not to see evil. Isaac's
payoff was tasty venison provided by Esau and, in fulfillment of Exodus 23:8, the bribe blinded the clear-
sighted.

Though bribes can take many forms, our disregard
of evil often stems from more subtle causes. Looking
the other way can simply become a habit; it may begin

with overlooking aggravating sights and escalate to ignoring moral monstrosities. Having initially tolerated the idolatrous incense-burning of Esau's wives, Isaac was gradually blinded by the smoke and nearly designated the fiend as his successor.

Another rabbinic interpretation traces Isaac's blindness back to his harrowing encounter with near-death at the hands of his father. Just before God called out to Abraham to spare his bound son, tears from the eyes of distraught angels fell into Isaac's eyes, damaging them forever. Isaac—the archetypical survivor—carries the trauma with him, blindly preferring brute strength over pious mildness when choosing the future leader of his people.

There are numerous reasons why good people, sometimes we ourselves, fail to see evil. Some may be found in the biblical and rabbinic portrayals of Isaac—if we just examine them with vision.

TRICKERY'S PRICE

Vayetze: Genesis 28:10–32:3

Yeshayahu Leibowitz

"Jacob went out," says Genesis 28:10. With what did he leave his father's house to go into exile? With the birthright and the blessing he had acquired by round-about and partly tricky means. But beyond the mission that had devolved on him as heir to the covenant of Abraham and Isaac, he had nothing. "With my staff I crossed the Jordan," he would testify twenty years later (Genesis 32:11).

The first great event after he left his home was the dream that for him, and for many generations of students and interpreters of the Torah after him, contained profound allusions of faith. After he awoke, Jacob took a vow that is surprising for a number of reasons.

First, after being granted this revelation of God, which included the promise of a glorious future, Jacob seems to speak only of satisfying his material needs of "bread to eat and clothing to wear" and of a happy return to his father's house (Genesis 28:20–21). Moreover, it

27

seems as if he set a condition for belief in God: if his wants were granted, then God would be his God.

But the great believers among the interpreters of the Torah explain this in an entirely different way. Jacob did not impose any condition for acceptance of faith in God. "God will be my God" (Genesis 28:21) was not a quid pro quo that Jacob promised, but was among the things he prayed for—bread, clothes, a return to his father's house, and that God should be his God.

More deeply, the midrash in *Breshit Rabbah* converts Jacob's vow from a request for supplying his needs to an obligation that he accepted upon himself toward God. Thus:

> *If God will be with me and protect me on the path* [Hebrew: *haderekh*] *I am going* means that He will preserve me from committing slander, as is said (Jeremiah 9:2), "They bend [Hebrew: *vayidrekhu*, from the same root] their tongues for lies."
>
> *and He will give me bread to eat* means that He will preserve me from sexual transgression, in accordance with the understanding that "the bread he eats" (Genesis 39:6) alludes to sex.
>
> *and I return in peace to my father's house* means I will refrain from bloodshed.
>
> *and He will be my God* means He will protect me from committing idolatry.

Jacob was not seeking to have his needs taken care of, but wanted God's help for fulfilling his obligation to abstain from slander, murder, lewdness, and idolatry.

But the midrash delves even deeper into this matter, in a way almost frightening. It asks: What caused Jacob to reach a state of having nothing, of having to beg for bread and clothing, of being in great distress and great danger and having to beg for protection? The reason was that he had obtained the birthright and the blessing by devious means, and as a result earned the enmity of his brother Esau and was forced to flee from his wrath and go into exile.

Here the same midrash makes a shocking statement: "All the things that Jacob wished to refrain from came upon him. He wished to refrain from slander, and what happened to him and his household? 'Joseph brought to his father their evil report' (Genesis 37:2). Jacob wished to refrain from lewdness, and in his household the affairs of Reuben and Bilhah, and of Judah and Tamar took place (Genesis 35:22; 38:1–30). He very much wished to live in peace and to refrain from shedding blood, and the affair of Shechem and Simeon and Levi occurred." Jacob's family, the midrash says, did all that he wished to avoid: slander, lewdness, shedding of blood, even idolatry—Rachel took her father's idols into Jacob's home (Genesis 31:19), and later Jacob had to demand that his children remove the foreign gods "in their midst" (Genesis 35:2,4).

Here we see that God does not show partiality even to His chosen ones. That is why the Chosen One of the forefathers (as Jacob is commonly known), who fulfilled the heavenly mission assigned to him, suffered all these failures: on his way to fulfill his mission, he did not follow the straight path.

Rape and Judgment

Vayishlah: Genesis 32:4–36:43

Bonna Devora Haberman

Dinah is the only daughter of our patriarch Israel. Dinah's own voice is silent in the text; after *Vayishlah*, she disappears into the void of an unwritten story, never to be heard of again. Though her name derives from *din*, "judgment," there is no verdict written in the Torah about her actions or her life. But, tradition says, the world will not stand on *din* alone. Though Dinah is mute, her chapter of violence and brutality cries out the need for *hesed*, "loving-kindness," to sustain life.

Dinah, we are told, "went out to see the daughters of the land" (Genesis 34:1). When Shechem sees her, "he takes her, lies with her, and rapes her" (Genesis 34:2). The climax of the series of violent events that ensues is the murder of all the males in Shechem's city. Ramban emphatically condemns the rape. But commentators also try to reveal the unstated cause of the calamities; some hold Dinah responsible. Midrash *Tanhuma* presumes Dinah must have been breaking

31

some halakhic restriction, such as carrying on *Shabbat*, when she ventured out; that transgression caused her downfall. Midrash *Tanhuma* also incriminates her as a woman: By "going out," a woman creates an opportunity for someone to transgress. She ought to have remained inside to avoid bringing misfortune on herself and others.

Another midrash, *Breshit Rabbati*, suggests that Dinah is identified as the "daughter of Leah" (Genesis 34:1) because she, like her mother, "goes out." Leah, the midrash explains, "went out" (Genesis 30:16) to meet Jacob after she and Rachel agreed that he would stay with Leah. Since both women "went out," the midrash assumes that the connection exists. Indeed, both incidents did end in sexual encounter.

The association is strengthened by the fact that the birth of Dinah is recounted four verses later. According to *Breshit Rabbah*, Leah prayed to change the gender of the fetus. If Dinah had been a boy, Rachel would have been left to bear only one son of the promised twelve. Leah did not want to lessen her sister's status. Dinah, then, was intended to be male—and so was inclined to "go out."

Most of these interpretations offend us. A woman, a person, is not to be taken, asserts my eight-year-old daughter. A woman leaving the private domain of her home to enter the public realm is not inciting sexual aggression. The rape victim is not to blame. This is an extreme case of gender stereotyping—and of unjustified judgement.

In contrast to the rape, the ex post facto portrayal of Shechem's affection for Dinah is one of the moving statements of love in the Torah. "His soul was drawn to Dinah, Jacob's daughter; and he loved her and spoke to her heart" (Genesis 34:3). Could she, does she, accept his repentance and love him?

Shechem and his father Hamor undergo circumcision to become acceptable to Jacob's family. Yet in spite of Shechem's love, the pattern of violence seems irrevocable. That there is a link between the rape and the demand for circumcision is certain: the male sex organ must be made fit for intercourse. The ineffectuality of retroactive circumcision necessitates the violent outcome. Simon and Levi, Dinah's brothers, attack the city, murdering every male. Was this not a continuation of the cutting they had inflicted three days before and of the cycle of violence that began with the rape? Surely circumcision must express a desire to participate in God's covenant. Without that pure motivation, circumcision became yet another violent act in the brutal sequence.

We never learn of Dinah's response, perhaps her destitution, after the murder of Shechem. Love was rendered impotent by the violence with which it began, and overshadowed by the brutality that irrevocably ended it. This, I suggest, was an implicit judgement against Dinah: silenced by rape.

Dinah was a child of Israel. Like her and her family, we face challenges concerning relationships among men and women and concerning how to conduct ourselves morally in the midst of other peoples. Perhaps Dinah's name is a statement of the potential of even one violent act between two individuals to create a cruel and untempered judgment that festers and infects. The world will not stand on *din*, judgement. We need to nurture the *hesed*, the love.

Unchain My Heart

Vayeshev: Genesis 37:1–40:23

Moshe Zemer

There is a strange digression in the Joseph story: between the false report of Joseph's death and his arrival in Egypt comes a riveting tale of domestic strife and extramarital goings-on.

Judah (Joseph's brother) has a son, Er, who dies, leaving a childless wife, Tamar. Judah commands his second son Onan to take Tamar in marriage "and provide offspring for your brother." Onan refuses to father Tamar's child—defiantly spilling his seed—and also dies. Tamar waits for Shelah, the third brother, to come of age. But then, despairing of securing her status within the family, she disguises herself as a harlot and tricks her father-in-law Judah into fathering her child.

The story provides the first example in the Bible of levirate marriage, *yibbum* in Hebrew, which has retained an important role in Jewish marriage law up to the present day. Biblical law laid down that a childless widow should be married to her brother-in-law. If he refused, a ceremony of release (*halitzah*) was performed before the elders of the city. As described in Deuteronomy 25:5-10, the widow removed her brother-in-law's sandal and spat in his face. Maimonides, explaining this "ancient custom" in *Guide to the Perplexed*, said the very "disgrace" of the rite was necessary to induce the man to marry his dead brother's wife. The widow had three alternatives: *yibbum*, *halitzah*—or remaining "chained" (an *agunah*) to her brother-in-law and unable to remarry. For centuries, rabbinic Sages debated whether levirate marriage or *halitzah* should be preferred. The controversy was resolved in 1950 by a ruling of Israel's Chief Rabbinic Council, strictly prohibiting levirate marriage. *Halitzah* has now been reduced to a rite of non-fulfillment of a forbidden act.

But for some childless widows, the problem has not been solved. They can remain "chained" for years to vindictive or unscrupulous brothers-in-law who demand extortionate sums in exchange for their release. Others must wait until a brother-in-law attains the age of *bar mitzvah*. And even when the man willingly complies, all parties to the ceremony usually find it as humiliating and "disgraceful" as Maimonides described.

Even though a man may not be formally coerced into *halitzah*, halakhic means were found at times to free these "chained" women. The Talmud states that in certain circumstances an unwilling brother-in-law can be tricked into *halitzah*. Some later rabbis approved adding conditions to the traditional betrothal formula that would retroactively annul the marriage if the bride later became a childless widow—thereby eliminating the need for *halitzah*. The sixteenth-century chief rabbi of Safed, Moshe Galante, wrote a responsum about a woman who ambushed her recalcitrant brother-in-law in the synagogue and spat before him in public. Galante ruled that although not valid *halitzah*, it made the woman ineligible for *yibbum*. So, he said, the brother-in-law must be forced to release her.

In Israel, there are at least twenty or thirty cases a year of women requesting *halitzah*. In wartime, this number can multiply many-fold. If refused, the woman's only recourse is civil marriage abroad (there is no civil marriage in Israel) or living with the man of her choice in common-law marriage. Non-Orthodox rabbis no longer require *halitzah* for remarriage—but this solution, again, is only available abroad.

Rabbinical courts in Israel have the power to impose sanctions, such as jail sentences or heavy maintenance payments, against men who stubbornly refuse *halitzah*. But these are of no avail if the brother-in-law is a minor or if he skips the country. Take the case of the twenty-three-year-old war widow whose brother-in-law, living in Germany, refused her *halitzah*, arguing that if not for her, his brother would have emigrated and remained alive.

Given the boldness of past solutions and the availability of halakhic mechanisms to overcome the need for *halitzah*, it is tragic that a biblical concern for the widow can cause her years of anguish, preventing her finding happiness with a new partner.

THE RISE OF JOSEPH JACOBSON

Miketz: Genesis 41:1–44:17

Gershom Gorenberg

Everyone has met someone like him: the kid who dreamt of getting ahead as he built towers in the sandbox; the boy who gave out ranks to the neighborhood children and made himself general; the young guy whom you called "ambitious" on good days and "climber" on bad; the man whose picture you saw years later in the paper—financial wizard, cabinet member, star.

Such is Joseph. As a boy, he sought his father's favor by snitching on his brothers. The reward, that coat, was an old-fashioned symbol of royalty, and so a promise of who would be king among the sons of Israel. He lived on the vertical axis, climbing, falling, and climbing higher. In Egypt, he was the original penniless immigrant who made good. The boss liked him, says Genesis 39:4, "and put all he had in his hands." A prison warden "put all the prisoners in his hand" (Genesis 39:22). "I've put you over all Egypt" (Genesis 41:41), says Pharaoh. Rather than *Joseph and His Broth-*

39

ers, a novel about him should be called *The Rise of Joseph Jacobson*, following Abraham Cahan's classic story of the Jew who made it in America, *The Rise of David Levinsky*.

Joseph was, as Arthur Waskow wrote in *Godwrestling*, always Number Two, "appointed to his power by someone yet more powerful." Not king, then, but court Jew. A man with a precarious position who was willing to help his brothers, he became the model for Mordechai and Esther, court bankers in Istanbul and Germany, men and women today who belong to the right party and can put in the right word. He was an archetype for generations of Exile—the more so because his power was ephemeral, and the rise of a king "who knew not Joseph" was bad news for us all.

He was an archetype in another sense, as literary critic Leslie Fiedler suggested in his essay "Master of Dreams: The Jew in a Gentile World." Joseph was the original Jewish peddler, and solver, of dreams: "the successful poet and the respected shrink." In our world, he has been split in two, Fiedler said: Kafka, the dreamer (who named his character Joseph K.), and Freud, who interpreted dreams. He was the model for a people hawking (or said to hawk) fantasy and abstraction, "love philters, liquid capital, cut diamonds . . . Hollywood movies," wrote Fiedler, who could have added theories of relativity to his list.

A man we might respect, even honor—but what makes Joseph a religious figure worthy of a quarter of Genesis? True, he turned down Potiphar's wife—though, as Rashi commented, he got her started, preening himself the moment her husband promoted him. But then, who could be more religious? To the seductress, fellow prisoners, Pharaoh, he spoke of God. He regarded dreams as Divine orders. He made sure all eleven brothers bowed to him, fulfilling his youthful vision, before revealing himself. He forgave them for selling him, because "it was not you that send me here, but God" (Genesis 45:8).

And that style of religiosity is what irks. Who needs this overweening talk of God before the unbelievers, this certainty he knows God's plan, this erasing of human responsibility? Who needs a man willing to serve Pharoah because he's sure he is serving God?

In the end, it seems, Jacob had similar doubts. In Genesis 49, we read his deathbed testament to his sons. Underlying it is the assumption that each son will live on, embodied in the tribe he founds. Jacob assigns kingship not to Joseph, but to Judah: a man who speaks rarely of God and never of vision, who lives on the horizontal axis of brothers—peers—and obligations to them. No unblemished saint, as a young man he sold a brother into slavery; not burdened by pride, he can say publicly of a woman he has wronged (Genesis 38:26): "She is more righteous than I." Grown older, he slips into leadership without seeking it when he says of his brother Benjamin, "I take responsibility for him" (Genesis 43:9). Despite Joseph's boyhood dreams, despite the promise made with a royal coat, Jacob tells Judah: "Your father's sons will bow down to you"—and thereby tells us who, in the tangled story of Joseph, is worthy of our honor.

MEMBER OF THE CLAN

Vayigash: Genesis 44:18–47:27

Avigdor Shinan

The climax has come in the drama of Joseph and his brothers: after a long speech in which Judah volunteers to remain in Egypt as Joseph's slave—thereby atoning for his decisive role in selling Joseph into slavery— Joseph "could no longer control himself" (Genesis 45:1) and tearfully tells his brothers: "I am Joseph."

His brothers are dumbfounded, until Joseph tells them to come nearer and repeats: "I am your brother Joseph." Then he reminds them of how they sold him into slavery in Egypt, and speaks of their father. He concludes with yet another attempt to convince them: "Your eyes see . . . that it is I who am speaking to you."

Joseph's threefold effort to prove his identity indicates the brothers' extreme distrust of what they were hearing. They sent a seventeen-year-old boy to Egypt and now face a thirty-nine-year-old man (whose beard, Rashi notes, had grown in that time); in place of a slave they confront the king's viceroy. And indeed, why should they trust the Egyptian, who had already treated them cruelly? Couldn't he be trying to catch them in new accusations? Recounting Joseph's sale is no proof; their lost brother may have told his story to some Egyptian, from whom it reached other ears.

So talmudic-era sources add two more signs by which Joseph sought to prove who he was: "It is I who am speaking to you" is rendered, in the Aramaic translation attributed to Yonatan ben Uziel, as "I am speaking to you in the holy tongue." Until now, in fact, the brothers had spoken to Joseph through an interpreter, with no sign that he understood Hebrew. The same Aramaic text then renders "Come forward to me" (Genesis 45:4) as "Come closer and see my circumcision."

A famous scene in the *Odyssey* portrays Odysseus's return to his home. Only his old nursemaid identifies him, after she washes his feet and notices a childhood scar on his leg. The midrash of *Ekhah Rabbah* (on Lamentations) tells a story of a brother and sister of a priestly family who fell into Roman captivity in their youth and were each sold into slavery. Years later their owners meet and decide to marry them. When the two are put in a room to consummate the match— which would inadvertently lead to incest—a conversation brings them to discover each other's identity. The brother convinces his sister of who he is by telling of their childhood home and by showing her a mole on his shoulder. The shared motif in the stories is the hidden bodily sign that confirms identity. The Aramaic translator and other rabbinic commentators added that motif to the story of Joseph and his brothers, and with it the matter of shared language.

It's clear that the rabbis regarded circumcision and the use of Hebrew as signs identifying fellow Jews within a foreign and hostile world. In the Hellenic– Roman world, the context for much of rabbinic literature, non-Jews regarded circumcision as barbaric and disgusting, and certainly only Jews spoke Hebrew. To these two signs we can add the one that Torah itself lets Joseph use: knowing the family and its past.

Hebrew, circumcision, and knowledge of a shared past were among a Jew's identity badges in the ancient world, but not open ones. The dress seen by all can fit gentile fashions; language reveals its truth only when it is spoken. One's bodily appearance may be the same as other people's; a part of the body hidden by modesty reveals one's roots. The present is shared with the general society; history points to one's uniqueness. Anyone who wants to fade into his surroundings can conceal his circumcision, avoid Hebrew, and not mention his people's past. But the signs are available when it comes time to identify oneself to other Jews, like members of a secret society.

The symbolism goes further: circumcision is an example of the religious commandments; Hebrew stands for shared culture; the family's past stands for national history. And so Joseph, the brother lost and regained, points to the three strands of shared identity for his people's future.

CALCULATED, NOT ACCIDENTAL

Veyehi: Genesis 47:28–50:26

W. Gunther Plaut

The modern world is fascinated with numbers. In most countries people are assigned numbers for many purposes of identification—passports, checks, social entitlements, or home addresses. A newspaper may tell us that X.Y., aged seventy-seven, received the Israel Prize; when someone dies, his or her age is always noted. Numbers are our specialty; they suffuse modern life.

The ancients were not altogether different. They, too, found numbers to be hooks upon which to hang one's recognition of others, and numbers served, as they do today, as an important part of the historical record. The Bible is, in this respect, much like other repositories of memory: It usually tells us how old the patriarch, king, or leader was when the Angel of Death called.

However, there is one key difference, especially in Genesis, which reaches its conclusion in this Torah portion: biblical numbers frequently convey a message. So it is with Jacob, of whom Genesis 47:28 reports

47

that he was 147 years old when he died. Earlier we were told that his father Isaac was 180 years at his death, and that his grandfather Abraham reached the age of 175. Whether or not these figures record the "actual" life span of the patriarchs, they relate an important truth.

Now the succession 175 (Abraham)—180 (Isaac)—147 (Jacob) does not at first glance seem to reveal anything, but that is only so because we moderns are no longer as intuitively attuned to numbers as were the ancients, who saw these figures as a pattern, and did so without having experience with the nomenclature that we learn in school. Thus:

$$175 = 5^2 \times 7$$
$$180 = 6^2 \times 5$$
$$147 = 7^2 \times 3$$

Still, there is no evidence that the biblical storyteller knew of squared numbers; and we might ask how the readers or hearers could understand this sequence. The answer—difficult as it may be for moderns to accept—is that the ancients had a holistic apprehension of numbers, while we approach mathematics in a fragmentary manner. We break down a problem, then put it together again; our forebears would look at the same puzzle as a whole. Not that all moderns have lost this sense: a high school student in Atlanta who heard me give the figures 175—180 concluded at once that 147 was "obviously" the next in sequence. My late father had a similar ability, though he had only a limited mathematical education.

In biblical days, not all listeners may have understood the message, but I think there were enough who did: that the patriarchs' lives were not accidental happenings but were planned by the Almighty.

The scheme goes further. Add the squared columns and you get 110, which is the number of years that

Joseph lived (Genesis 50:26), a hint that Joseph was the true successor of his forebears. The counterpart of Joseph, who took the children of Israel out of the Promised Land, is Joshua, who brought them back. He dies, like Joseph, at 110, an obvious and divinely planned parallel (Joshua 24:29).

Between Joseph and Joshua stands Moses, who lived to 120, which was considered the perfect age, for it is built into the structure of the human body. Our hands have five fingers; multiply them and you get:

$$1 \times 2 \times 3 \times 4 \times 5 = 120$$

There are numerous other numbers with a message. For instance, Noah's days had a "cosmic" dimension: He died at age 950, which is 50 x 19. Nineteen years is the period it takes for the sun, earth, and moon to return to the exact same positions in the sky; for this reason, the Jewish calendar is built on a nineteen–year cycle. Methusaleh, the oldest figure in antedeluvian chronology, lived another nineteen years, to 969.

Modern bibilical scholar Nahum Sarna put it well, therefore, when he said that these chronologies "constitute paradigmatic rather than pragmatic history." To call attention to these numbers is not an exercise in *gematria*, the rabbinic attempt to find hidden meanings in words by adding the numerical value of their letters and comparing them to words of like value (*alef* = 1, *beit* = 2, *gimel* = 3). The numbers above were not hidden. They were clearly written into the text as part of its original intention and conveyed to the ancients the message of God's role in the formation of His people.

It was an important message which modern readers do well to recover: We are not accidents of history, but children of the covenant, which links us and our lives inextricably to the Divine.

EXODUS

My Brother, My Victim

Shmot: Exodus 1:1–6:1

Deborah Weissman

The exodus of Hebrew slaves from Egypt, under the leadership of Moses, might have been the first social revolution in human history. The biographical sketch of Moses with which the story begins is an apt prelude: it mentions three incidents in his early life that illustrate his sense of justice and identification with the oppressed.

One of the world's foremost Bible teachers, Nehama Leibowitz of Jerusalem, wrote this about these incidents, as described in Exodus 2:11–22:

> Moses intervened on three occasions to save the victim from the aggressor. Each of these represents an archetype. First, he intervenes in a clash between a Jew and a non-Jew; second, between two Jews; and third, between two non-Jews. In all three cases, Moses championed the just cause. Any further clash must needs belong to one of these three categories.

An interesting observation, but not entirely accurate: the possibility of a fourth archetype, in which the Jew is oppressor and the non-Jew the victim, apparently did not occur to Leibowitz, writing several decades ago—nor, apparently, to Jewish readers of the Torah throughout the ages. Their experience undoubtedly underscored their perception of the Jew as victim. Today's Israeli reality may show that Jews can be victimizers as well as victims.

In the first archetype, the Egyptian is the oppressor, whom Moses kills, and the Hebrew slave the victim. Strikingly, a midrash attributes the fact that Moses is not permitted to enter the Promised Land to his killing of the Egyptian. The taking of a human life, even that of an evil adversary, is perceived as wrong—necessary perhaps in self-defense, but still ultimately wrong. Ruling out a pacifist approach, which I think is alien to mainstream Jewish tradition, how are we to understand this sensitivity?

Sometimes sources in which we might least expect to find them give us valuable insights—in this case, a humanistic spiritual insight from an eighteenth-century hasidic master, basing himself on kabbalistic texts on the transmigration of souls.

Rabbi Aharon of Karlin comments on the ambiguity in Exodus 2:11 ". . . and he saw an Egyptian smiting a Hebrew, one of his brethren." The question arises, to whom does "his brethren" refer? Is the Hebrew one of Moses's brethren—or possibly, one of the Egyptian's brethren? Can an Egyptian and a Hebrew be considered brothers? And does this mean that the Egyptian and Moses were brothers?

Drawing upon earlier mystical traditions, the Karliner says that Abel's soul was reincarnated in Moses, while Cain's became the Egyptian he smote. One does not have to accept the kabbalistic theory of reincarnation to derive meaning from this approach. I would offer two understandings:

The first portion in Genesis relates the story of Cain and Abel, the first homicide, which was also a fratricide. Symbolically, *Shmot*, the first portion in Exodus, also describes a fratricide. Perhaps this teaches that all killing is, essentially, the killing of brothers and sisters.

Moses' killing of the Egyptian can be viewed as retribution for the murder of Abel. The score has been settled; the blood feud must end.

During the French Revolution, the story goes, the mistress of the house asked her maidservant, "What is this thing you call revolution?" to which the latter replied, "Revolution means that I will become the mistress of the house and you will become the maidservant."

The Exodus Revolution, which Moses led, cannot simply mean that former slaves themselves become oppressors. The Exodus message of human liberation from oppression must be founded on a vision of humankind as brethren, all created in God's image, all equally worthy of life.

LIBERATION, THEN THEOLOGY
Va'era: Exodus 6:2-9:35

Irving Greenberg

The promise of freedom is fourfold: "I will take you out from under the burdens of Egypt; and I will save you from their slavery; and I will redeem you . . . and I will take you to be My people." But take note of what is to happen when the Divine pledges are fulfilled: "Then you will know that I am the Lord your God" (Exodus 6:6-7).

Overcoming oppression and cruelty, ending war and slavery—nothing less will establish the credibility of God. Neither spirituality nor teaching about transcendence will have lasting validity as long as human misery remains rampant.

This wedding of history and faith is articulated by Pharaoh and God alike. The tyrant makes the connection in his scornful reply to Moses' plea to release the Israelite slaves: "I do not know of God—and I will not send Israel out" (Exodus 5:3).

When Pharaoh tightens the vise by cutting off the supply of straw to the slaves while demanding they meet their full production quota of bricks, Moses and the Hebrews are crushed. Then God speaks, using the name YHWH, which is normally translated "the Lord" so that it will not be pronounced: "I am YHWH. I appeared to Abraham, to Isaac, to Jacob by my name El Shaddai; but by My name YHWH I was not known to them" (Exodus 6:3).

Modern Bible critics argue that this verse reveals a tradition that YHWH was not the God of the patriarchs, but one who emerged in a later era. Traditional commentaries provide a theologically deeper approach. Says Rashi: "It does not say 'I did not make My name known to them' (Hebrew, *lo hodati*), but rather 'I was not known to them' (*lo nodati*)." God's name YHWH was revealed many times to the patriarchs, but it was "known" only as a word because God's redemption remained a promise and not yet a deed.

As long as the patriarchs remained landless outsiders, as long as the Israelites remained slaves, they did not really know God as God. In Hebrew, to know means to experience totally; it refers to knowledge that goes from the brain to the gut. The same term, "to know," is used for sexual intercourse. In earthly and Divine love alike, one "knows" the other with body and soul, as undeniably, totally present.

In the presence of war and degradation, talk of God is only talk. True, the hungry and exploited call out to God. But in their suffering they experience God, not as Loving Presence, but as a straw to be grasped at. To spread the knowledge of God, one must be a liberator, a caretaker, and protector of orphans, widows, and strangers.

The prophetic judgment is relentless. Those who preach religion but shun activism—or worse, deny justice—turn talk of God into empty rhetoric. Unethical "pious" people show by their behavior that their God is only a smoke screen for crime ("Even when you make many prayers, I will not listen because your hands are full of blood," says Isaiah 1:15, and see verses 11–17). Established religions that accommodate the state by blessing an unjust status quo do not know God. Those who persecute or kill in the name of God are "desecrators of the Divine Name," degraders of God's image from that of a redeeming force to a mask for murderers.

When the Holocaust removed God's presence because history had become so cruel, creating the State of Israel provided a measure of redemption, which made God more "present" in the world. Paradoxically, it was secular Jews as much as observant Jews who acted to restore the image of God by providing better care and dignity for Jews and all humans. While rabbis of all denominations went on praying—saying all the right words about God—as if nothing had happened, it remained for "secularists" (and "modern" Orthodox) to join the army and give their lives in disproportionate numbers to establish the State of Israel.

Who then truly spreads the knowledge of God? Actions speak louder than words. And when will that knowledge be complete? When, as Isaiah promised (Isaiah 11:9), the world becomes God's holy mountain: "They will do no harm and stop all destruction on My holy mountain, then the earth will be full of knowledge of God as the waters cover the sea."

SIGN ON THE DOOR

Bo: Exodus 10:1–13:16

Fredelle Z. Spiegel

We have entered the realm of signs, of a theological street theater in which both set and action are meant to point beyond themselves. There are signs to Pharaoh to demonstrate God's supremacy so that he will free the people of Israel; signs to the Israelites so that they will remember the Exodus and observe God's commandments.

In the portion of *Bo*, we have also reached the Torah's first significant collection of commandments, one that is generally divided into three categories: the laws of observing the first Passover; the directive to set apart firstborn animals for God and to redeem firstborn sons; and the command to have a sign upon your hand and a memorial between your eyes (Exodus 13:9; 13:16) that came to be the *mitzvah* of *tefillin*. Like the plagues, these *mitzvot* all deal in the highly visual.

The Israelites' ritual observances are all meant to be conspicuous, ordained specifically so that the quintessential Jewish question will be asked: Why this? They are meant to serve as reminders of God's work. They offer the occasions to tell children about the Exodus (verses 12:26–27; 13:8, and 13:14 provide the questions and answers for three of the *Haggadah*'s four sons). The community's members observe the rituals of the Passover meal and place signs and memorials on their bodies.

In perhaps the most extraordinary visualization, even certain members of the community, the firstborn sons, themselves become reminders of the Exodus. For on the night that the Egyptian's firstborn were slain, God saved the Israelites' sons. And the story of this deliverance contains yet another sign: the Israelites must place blood around their doors, "and the blood shall be to you for a sign upon the houses where you are; and when I see the blood, I will pass over you and there shall no plague be upon you to destroy you" (Exodus 12:13). Again, in Exodus 12:23, "For the Lord will pass through to smite the Egyptians; and when He sees the blood upon the lintel, and on the two side-posts, the Lord will pass over the door, and will not suffer the destroyer to come in unto your houses to smite you."

The need to mark the Israelite homes to avoid the tenth plague stands in marked contrast to the story of the ninth plague. When there was darkness in the homes of the Egyptians, "all the children of Israel had light in their dwellings" (Exodus 10:23). God was able to distinguish between the households without any help from their inhabitants.

The midrash, in the early collection known as the *Mekhilta*, emphasizes the construction in verse 13: "the blood shall be to you for a sign," explaining that the sign was not for God, but for the Israelites themselves. The medieval philosopher Maimonides notes that slaying sheep was forbidden in Egypt; so in killing the lamb to get the blood, the Israelites were freeing themselves from pagan culture.

Yet it seems that there is more to this requirement of marking the Israelite houses, for it is consistent with one of the leitmotifs of this portion: the commands to teach one's children of God and the Exodus. For the slaves who were freed that night the only way to be able to teach their children was first to insure that their children survived the plague. Marking their dwellings was the prerequisite to fulfilling all of the educational commandments.

For our generation, the need to mark our homes is even greater. We, too, must teach our children of the Exodus and we, too, must begin in the same way. As it was for our ancestors, the first step for us is to insure Jewish survival. And, just as for the generation who left Egypt, we, too, must begin by marking our dwellings as distinctly Jewish. If we have homes in which Jewish rituals are not noticeably observed, homes without a *mezuzah* on the door or books of Jewish learning within, our children will not have the opportunity to ask the Jewish questions of "What is this?" or even the rebellious son's standoffish "What does this service mean to you?" There will be no daily occasions to be reminded of the Exodus.

We no longer need signs for Pharaoh; we need them for ourselves.

BIG-DEAL MIRACLE
Beshallah: Exodus 13:17–17:16

Hillel Halkin

"A hasty people," *ama peziza*, the Talmud calls us, on the basis of the book of Exodus, and we haven't changed much since then. "Nervous," "quicktempered," "contentious," "impulsive," "overexpectant," "ungrateful," "impatient," "undisciplined," "demanding," "high-strung," "easily disappointed"—any of these adjectives still fits us as snugly as it does the Israelites who followed Moses out of Egypt. Can it be only a few short years since the Russian and Ethiopian exoduses, now considered emblems of national failure, were euphorically hailed as Zionist fairy tales come true? That's not even close to the record:

"Then sang Moses and the children of Israel this song unto the Lord, and spake, saying, I will sing unto the Lord, for He hath triumphed gloriously" (Exodus 15:1). "And the whole congregation of the children of Israel murmured against Moses in the wilderness . . . Would to God we had died by the hand of the Lord in the land of Egypt when we sat by the fleshpots and when we

did eat bread to the full! For you have brought us forth
unto this wilderness to kill this whole assembly with
hunger" (Exodus 16:23). Estimated time lapse between
the two events: a month and a half.

One might think that the impact of the miracle at the
Red Sea would have lasted a bit longer, but there's
really no reason why it should have. You can't fill
today's empty stomach with yesterday's miracle, and
what is a miracle anyway? It is somebody else's coincidence, and the Bible, which is not overly modest
about God's role in things, makes the point clear in this
case. "And Moses stretched out his hand over the sea;
and the Lord caused the sea to go back by a strong east
wind all night, and made the sea dry land, and the
waters were divided." You could call it the work of the
Lord and you could call it a freak wind, and it is fair to
assume that the hungrier the children of Israel became
in the desert, the more they inclined toward the second hypothesis.

One of the uncanny things about the Bible is the way
it repeats upon us Jews. Other peoples have their national epics and some of these are great literature, but
I doubt that any Greek is ever seized by the odd feeling that whole lines of "The Iliad" have been plagia-
rized from the morning newspaper. "And they said to
Moses: Were there not enough graves in Egypt that you
took us away to die in the wilderness? Why have you
done this to us, to take us out of Egypt?" It could be a
demonstration at one of Ariel Sharon's mobile-home
sites.

Even those of us with roofs over our heads don't
always see beyond them. Little problems hide big wonders. Try the following experiment. Suppose I were to
tell you that, as a Jew living in Israel, you are extraor-
dinarily privileged to be at the epicenter of one of the
greatest historical adventures ever participated in by
a people on earth—when would you be more likely to

smirk at me: in a month when life has been treating you well, or in one when the bank wants its overdraft back, the car needs an overhaul, and your child brings home a bad report card? We all know that our personal fortunes are no criteria for judging the universe, but in one way or another this is exactly how we judge it and we would not be human if we didn't.

Let us not be too hard on those unregenerate Israelites in the desert. In some ways, we're rather like them and we're not such a bad lot. At least they stuck it out and did not go back to Egypt, which is more than can be said for some people we know. It's easiest to overlook a miracle when it's all around you—"on your right hand and on your left," as *Beshallah* puts it.

HANDS OFF OF NATURE!

Yitro: Exodus 18:1–20:26

Jeremy Benstein

The Sabbath appears out of place in the Ten Commandments. It is the only ritual requirement in the bunch. Tucked in between the first three commandments, which deal with monotheism and idolatry, and the following six, which regulate relations between people, *Shabbat* is connected to both categories yet fully part of neither. It is among the best known Jewish practices, and one of the least understood. We are commanded to rest, yet nowhere is the meaning of rest spelled out in the written Torah. The rabbis, on the other hand, provide us with more details than we might care for. It becomes a violation to pick a flower, write a poem or, later on, flick a switch.

"Are we dealing here with extravagant and compulsive exaggerations of an originally 'sensible' ritual," psychoanalyst Erich Fromm wrote, "or is our understanding of the ritual perhaps faulty and in need of revision?" Fromm's answer was the latter, and he provided the following definition of what is forbidden on the seventh day: "'Work' is any interference by man, be it constructive or destructive, with the physical world. Rest is a state of peace between man and nature."

This *aggadah* of *Shabbat*, the theory behind the practice, is hinted at in the commandment itself: we rest in imitation of the original divine rest that was the climax and cessation of Creation. Yet God's rest allowed the world to exist without Divine intervention. In the same way, Shabbat is as much a respite for the world as it is for the people who observe it. How else can we understand a day of joy and rest that prohibits labor-saving devices, and involves frequent inconvenience—but by seeing that something other than human needs are paramount?

The link between the commandment and the creation story indicates how *Shabbat* rest contrasts with creative labor. Genesis describes a very anthropocentric world: humanity stands at the head of the created beings, as benevolent dictator in chapter 1, and conscientious steward in chapter 2. *Shabbat* implies an approach that can be labeled biocentric, demanding that humans abstain from domination. It thereby allows them to see themselves as creatures, rather than creators. Orthodox philosopher David Hartman says of the seventh day: ". . . the flowers of the field stand over and against man as equal members of the universe. I am forbidden to pluck the flower or to do with it as I please; at sunset the flower becomes a 'thou' to me with a right to existence regardless of its possible value for me . . . The Sabbath aims at healing the human grandiosity of technological society."

Shabbat, then, is to time what a nature preserve is to space. Both are "places" marked with distinct boundaries. In both, the soul of the human "visitor" is refreshed, while the natural order is preserved in its unviolated form. Outside the boundaries, we do not seek to negate civilization, the realm of human action, and make the whole world a preserve. But ideally the values experienced inside the "fence" will influence how we view the world beyond, and our role in it.

But there is an unresolved tension between the lofty *aggadah* and the nitty-gritty of the *Shabbat halakhah*. If *Shabbat* implies renouncing human domination over the natural world and represents a more harmonious relationship with the rest of creation, then how can we justify the waste involved in modern observance of the Sabbath, such as leaving lights and other electric appliances on for the entirety of the day? And doesn't Sabbath observance become a violation of the *mitzvah* of *bal tash'hit*—the prohibition of senseless waste?

Some observant Jews look to technology to solve the problem: let timers operate our lights; let us "observe" the Sabbath by using electronic relays and devices invented specifically for the seventh day. But is turning to technological innovations to comply with restrictions in the Sabbath's spirit of humility and human creatureliness? Rather, it only emphasizes our continued scientific exploitation of nature, and the use of the uniquely human creative impulse that we are meant to be restraining on this day. Perhaps there is no single solution that will satisfy all Jews, but I believe that the issue must be addressed when teaching, and observing, *Shabbat*.

THE CIVIL AND THE SPIRITUAL

Mishpatim: Exodus 21:1–24:18

Nachum L. Rabinovitch

Tensions between individual and society are as old as mankind. At times, the Torah addresses the balance between them in explicit terms; at times, the Torah's view emerges from the way it recounts events. *Mishpatim* illustrates both approaches.

"These are the ordinances which you shall set before them"—thus opens our reading, laying out the covenant between God and Israel. In precise phrases, it summarizes criminal and civil law, ranging from penalties for murder, assault, and theft to rules regulating relations between master and servant, lender and borrower, and finder and loser.

The last ten verses (Exodus 23:10–19) briefly survey what nowadays is called "religion"—exclusive worship of the one God; the obligations of the Sabbath, the sabbatical year, and the pilgrimage festivals; and the prohibition of certain foods.

This last "ritual" section is repeated almost verbatim later—when the covenant is renewed after the people break their compact with God and worship the golden calf (Exodus 34:17–26). Avraham Ibn Ezra, the medieval commentator, explains that these laws lay down the conditions that must be fulfilled if the the covenant between God and His people is to remain in force. That covenant allows every Jew to participate in the special relationship with God, which sustains the spirit and nourishes the soul.

The much larger body of law that constitutes the bulk of our Torah portion is addressed to the governing authorities. This section ends, according to Ibn Ezra, with the admonition to the judge, "You shall not oppress a stranger" (Exodus 23:9)—the judge must not favor an Israelite over a stranger.

Thus the legal system of Torah consists of two parts. One, the proper jurisdiction of the government, deals with affairs of society. The other—the commandments between man and God—belongs to every Jew.

This division has important implications. The rulers are charged with implementing the laws between man and his fellow men, and are granted wide legislative and administrative powers in this realm. True, a Jewish authority that dared to violate the Torah's norms of equity and justice would lose its right to govern. But legitimate government enjoys the sanction of the Torah in its rightful functions.

However, no Jewish government or king has any status at all with respect to what Ibn Ezra characterized as "the conditions of the covenant." The ultimate goals of spiritual welfare are to be achieved by means other than government. All the individuals comprising the public as a whole are expected to uphold the covenant. This duty may not and cannot be shifted to the rulers. Nor may the rulers arrogate to themselves any such powers.

Because of the hiatus of almost two thousand years in Jewish sovereignty, it is not surprising that these fundamental principles of Jewish law are not adequately recognized or are misunderstood and misapplied in our reborn state. Thus, some agitate for the Knesset to legislate a counterfeit civil substitute for Jewish marriage. Others demand so-called "religious legislation." Neither is in the Knesset's jurisdiction.

The Torah does not recognize any human institution as the ultimate, all-embracing authority. In matters where economic and spiritual factors overlap, government must cede to the individuals involved. Every individual is heir to both the challenge and the promise of the covenant: "You shall serve the Lord your God, and He will bless your bread and your water . . . I will fulfill the number of your days" (Exodus 23:26).

BEYOND THE SOVEREIGN SELF

Trumah: Exodus 25:1–27:19

Ed Greenstein

Modern times have moved us more and more toward personal and group autonomy. The Enlightenment gave us the will, and technology the means, to achieve relative independence. As nations turn increasingly self-reliant, individuals also seek self-sufficiency. Bookstores have self-help sections; a popular American magazine is tellingly titled *Self*; and many of us endeavor to be our own doctor, lawyer, and rabbi—even if we have occasional need for a personal trainer or shrink.

The splintering of our communities into individuals often strains the bond of group responsibility. In the political domain, Republicans in the U.S. whittle away at social sharing, even as the Israeli economy is privatized. The brutalities endemic to the further Balkanization of the Balkans prompt rhetoric of righteous condemnation and a policy of live and let live—as death follows death.

Within the Jewish community, concern grows over steady fragmentation into self-centered groupings.

Such division is often justified in the name of religious, political or social purity. But forming tight-knit communities within the larger group represents a kind of collective individualism, buttressed by a holier-than-thou attitude—an abundance of contemporary Qumrans, splendidly isolated communities that burn brightly until they spend their supply of spirit.

The religion of the Torah implies and often engenders a sense of dependency on God. At the same time, it recognizes the individual's legitimate spiritual needs; it also fosters an awareness of people's dependence on others. These perspectives are reflected in the two distinctive types of contributions that are levied to build the dwelling-place of God in the midst of the Israelite camp. The first type begins the portion of *Trumah*, the second begins *Ki Tissa*, read two weeks later. Together they bracket the Torah's instructions on how to build the sanctuary.

Surprisingly, the contribution mandated at the outset is entirely voluntary, to be made only by those whose hearts move them to do so (Exodus 25:2). God tells Israel to make their contributions "for Me." Individuals may choose whether to satisfy their personal aspirations through a donation to the Divine dwelling-place—but the purpose of the donation, as medieval commentators Rashi and Ralbag remark, is to serve God, not themselves. The very idea of housing God among the people as a continual source of protection and blessing underscores the dependency of people on a power greater than and outside of themselves.

The second contribution is that of the half-shekel. It functions to "ransom" the Israelites' lives. So everyone must pay it and, all lives being of equal worth, each payment must be half a shekel in weight, no more, no less (Exodus 30:12–13). The need for all to ransom their lives instills the notion that all are dependent on God's power. What's more, as the Italian Renaissance rabbi

Azariah Figo explained in his *Binah La'itim* ("Wisdom for Every Occasion"), the fact that each Israelite submits half a weight teaches us that the other half of one's weight is held by another Israelite—potentially, by every other Israelite. Just as we are dependent on God, we are interdependent on one another.

We are also responsible for each other. The Torah makes it clear in its description of the dwelling-place and its rituals that all Israelites must maintain the purity of the camp housing God's presence. Anyone's violations of that purity, regardless of intention, will temporarily remove the Divine from the community. The Torah's religion, which seeks in every way to insure that the community be fit for God's presence, insists that whatever one member of the community does affects everyone else. Consequences are shared, and so must be the responsibility.

The Torah provides a framework in which individuals can exercise a certain freedom. Contrary to the views of some, it makes room for individual expression. But that freedom must be balanced by acceptance of responsibility to and for one another.

DOWN TO THE LAST DETAIL

Tetzaveh: Exodus 27:20–30:10

Michael Rosenak

Why were our forefathers commanded to build a sanctuary? When? And why the endless details about the materials, the manner of its construction, and even the clothing to be worn in it by the priests?

Let's look at the "why" in the context of the "when." The midrash reconstructs the biblical chronological context to make the point that building the sanctuary was commanded the day after Yom Kippur in the year of exodus. That was *after* the golden calf *and after* Moses' second ascent to Sinai, to receive Divine forgiveness and new tablets of the covenant.

With this in mind, it has been suggested that the golden calf made the sanctuary necessary: the graven image expressed a yearning for concrete evidence of God's presence. After the extraordinary experience at Mount Sinai, Moses had left the camp to ascend into the mists of the mountain. The *Shekhinah*—as the Divine Presence is personified in Hebrew—had apparently vanished into thin air. Aaron, perhaps sympathizing with the Israelites' fear and sense of loss, gave in to their demand to fashion the gold and silver brought from Egypt into a graven image. Later, God, in a gesture of forgiveness and reconciliation, instructed them to use that wealth to make an acceptable symbol of His presence.

One midrash suggests that God merely *permitted* the building of the sanctuary. In this version, the Israelites plead that, just as all kings have trappings of sovereignty, so God should have them. God assures them that He needs no trappings and He promises to watch over them. But still they persist. God agrees, but on one condition—the sanctuary must be built exactly as He commands, down to the last detail.

Here, then, is a possible answer to the third question. The wealth of technical details, extending from the measurements of each item of the tabernacle to the minutiae of the high priest's garments, made the sanctuary and its service a *mitzvah*—a commandment—not only a psychological need. It was part of the Torah—not a heady substitute for it.

From its beginning, the Bible declares and describes the search of the divine and the human for each other. Adam and Eve hear God "walking in the garden" of Eden. The patriarchs and matriarchs pray and are answered. Then, in the years of Egyptian bondage, God seems to be no more than a ghostly memory, the silent "God of the fathers" until He "remembers" the children of Abraham, sends His servant Moses to deliver them and gives them the words of His covenant.

But the Israelites feel lost nonethless. Presence as moral code seems abstract and cold. True, they are going to the land God has promised them, but who knows what awaits them there? In the vast wilderness the liberation itself becomes grotesque, symbolizing only the loss of the familiar—like the cucumbers they were so fond of in Egypt.

The desire for God's presence, the Torah teaches us, is not only legitimate, but echoes God's own "wish" for humans He can love. This aspiration requires concreteness: in specific deeds, a real homeland and actual historical people.

But the yearning for presence is also explosive, dangerous. Building sanctuaries in the throes of spiritual fervor can be morally obtuse and insensitive, even when exciting and apparently meaningful. God commanded us to build a sanctuary—and understands that we need one, for otherwise we build golden calves. But there is a proviso: "If you insist," says the midrash, "then I insist that you make it as I command you"—lest it become, through untempered enthusiasm or bottomless dread, idolatrous.

And together with the outward, social symbol, one must cultivate inwardness. In the words of Malbim, the nineteenth-century exegete: "Make a sanctuary in the compartments of your heart, preparing yourself to be a dwelling place for the Divine Presence."

WHAT THE JEWS DO

Ki Tissa: Exodus 30:11–34:35

David Rosen

After the debacle of the golden calf, Moses pleads to
God to forgive the children of Israel. He also seeks a
profounder understanding of the Divine character to
serve as a guide to the people in their own behavior.

Moses is told that God's goodness will be revealed
to him, but "a human being cannot see God and live"
(Exodus 33:20). The revelation will be partial: "And you
shall see my back, but my face shall not be seen."

The traditional interpretation: God's "back"—the most
that we can know of God—refers to the thirteen Divine
attributes expressed in Exodus 34:6–7. God is described
as "merciful and gracious, long-suffering and abundant
in goodness . . ."

Elsewhere, the Torah's descriptions of God's qualities include those of vengeance and wrath. Yet only
the thirteen attributes are taught by our tradition as
constituting the essential Godly character, which we
should emulate. Abba Shaul sums it up in the early
midrashic text, the *Mekhilta*: "Just as He is gracious and

compassionate, so you be gracious and compassionate." Our Sages not only called the Jews "merciful ones,
the children of merciful ones," but declared that anyone lacking compassion was to be suspected of not
being a true Jew.

The thirteen attributes have a second, liturgical function. The Talmud, in Tractate *Rosh Hashanah*, declares
that through them God provided an eternal therapy
for Israel: "It is guaranteed for Israel that whenever
they sin, let them recite these thirteen attributes and
they will be forgiven."

As far as individuals are concerned, our Sages teach
that there is no atonement without prior contrition.
But from the talmudic statement, it appears that when
it comes to the people of Israel as a whole, God guar-
antees absolution, even without prior contrition. Why?

After the golden calf, Moses seeks forgiveness by
arguing: "Why should Egypt say that He took them out
with evil intent to destroy them . . ." (Exodus 32:12).
The argument is repeated after a later failure, when
the spies sent to the promised land returned with a
negative report (Numbers 14:16).

Moses' argument, which God accepts, is that because
Israel's very existence testifies to the Divine Presence
in history, Israel must not be destroyed. Yet the argument contains a corollary, which leads us back to the
function of the thirteen attributes as moral guide: because Israel's purpose is to testify to the Divine Presence in history, what the gentiles say and conclude
about Israel is of critical importance.

David Ben-Gurion's well-known remark, "It doesn't
matter what the goyim say. What matters is what the
Jews do," is in keeping with Jewish tradition—if it
means we must not let others' opinions prevent us
from doing what we believe to be right, just, and necessary. But people who understand it as contempt for
gentiles' conclusions about our behavior disregard a

fundamental Jewish teaching. For Judaism categori-
cally calls upon us to behave, individually and nation-
ally, in a way that elicits moral respect and thus sanc-
tifies God's name.

Say our Sages in *Seder Eliyahu Rabbah*: "See that you
are beloved by all human beings and keep far from sin,
bloodshed, and theft from Jew, heathen, or any person.
For he who sins against, spills the blood, or steals from
a non-Jew, will eventually sin against, spill the blood,
and steal from a Jew as well. Moreover, the Torah was
only given to sanctify God's name in the world. As it
is written: 'I will put a sign on them . . . and they shall
declare my glory among the gentiles'" (Isaiah 66:19).

THE FACE IN THE MIRROR

Vayakhel: Exodus 35:1–38:20

Susan Afterman

Because of the merit of righteous women in the generation of the Exodus, says Rabbi Akiba in the midrash
of *Shmot Rabbah*, Israel was redeemed from Egypt. And,
according to the same midrashic collection, when the
people of Israel, frightened by Moses' delay in returning from Mt. Sinai, decided to create a "substitute," the
golden calf, these women did not participate.

What made them capable of gaining this merit? A hint
may be found in the description of the laver (basin) for
the Tabernacle. The building of the Tabernacle, says the
midrash in both *Sifrei* and *Tanhuma*, was atonement
for and rectification of the sin of making the golden
calf. The laver and its base, to be made of brass, were
to be used by the priests to wash their hands and feet
before serving in the tabernacle, "that they die not"
(Exodus 30:20–21).

Vayakhel hints at why the laver and its water provided such protection. "And he made the laver of brass
and its pedestal of brass from the mirrors of women

89

crowding, who crowded at the door of the Tent of Meeting" (Exodus 38:8). Explaining the unusual repetition of "crowd" in the verse, Rashi comments, "The daughters of Israel owned mirrors that they looked in when they adorned themselves, and even these they did not refrain from donating to the Tabernacle. And Moses spurned them because they were made to serve the evil urge. But The Holy One, Blessed Be He, told him: 'Accept them, for they are more dear to Me than everything else. For it was through them that the women [gave birth to] whole crowds in Egypt.' When their husbands were exhausted from hard labor, the women would go and bring them food and drink. Then each would pick up her mirror, and see herself with her husband in the mirror, and would speak seductively to him . . . and arouse his desire, and come to him, and conceive and give birth. . . ."

But why were these mirrors chosen to hold the water with which the priests washed, "that they die not"? The priests faced two main dangers in their service. The first was that they might carry contamination into the Tabernacle from impurity they had suffered in their private lives. To counter this danger, they purified their hands and feet. The second was that their souls might, in the environment of revealed holiness, leave their bodies. They needed to be held, as the water they washed in needed to be held. The use of the mirrors for this purpose implies that the priests could be protected by being connected to the quality that had enabled the women both to affirm life so strongly in this world (as revealed in Rashi's startling comment) and to refrain from participating in the making of the golden calf.

This quality may be directly related to the process of looking into the mirror. Both the words for mirror in Hebrew, *re'i* and *mar'eh*, have their root in the verb "to see," *ra'ah*. To look into the mirror is to look for oneself, to see who one is. And who "I" am is, in the last analysis, ungraspable, unknowable, rooted ultimately in the Divine Nothingness, *Ein Sof*. This is what may be seen if one penetrates the passing images. On the other hand, the "I" who looks into the mirror is tangibly flesh and blood, something. These two opposite perceptions are locked together, neither capitulating to the other. And the ability to exist in this state, to hold and affirm the two opposite realities, is a property of faith.

It was perhaps this faith, this ability to endure contradiction and paradox, that made it seem worthwhile and desirable to bring children into a state of slavery and danger, and that made replacing Moses when he failed to return "on time" not seem imperative. It was this, for the righteous women of the Exodus generation, that made it possible to bear uncertainty, to wait and live.

THE MEDIUM IS NOT THE MESSAGE

Pekudei: Exodus 38:21–40:38

Mordechai Beck

The best known Jewish statement of principle on art is, unfortunately, the ban given at Sinai on making graven images with a likeness of "anything in the heavens above or the earth beneath" (Exodus 20:3). Despite this prohibition, a few chapters later the same jealous God commands Moses to erect a tabernacle and fill it with objects of beauty that are described with such precise detail as to suggest Divine acceptance of the power of the visual on the imagination of His children (Exodus 25–40). How do we explain this radical change of heart? Is art not only to be permitted but even lauded as a means of reaching the Divine?

The key to this riddle is found in the figure of Bezalel—or to give him his full name, as it appears when he is first mentioned and again at the beginning of *Pekudei*—"Bezalel, son of Uri, son of Hur, from the tribe of Judah" (Exodus 31:2, 38:22), who "made all that the Lord had commanded Moses." He was an artist and craftsman capable of fashioning objects that inspired awe, in the same way, perhaps, that the works of Leonardo and Michelangelo did for their contemporaries. Does this mean that God repented his objections to the visual image? What did Bezalel bring to his work that made it kosher?

According to Midrash *Tanhuma*, the answer lies in the very lineage mentioned in the Bible when Bezalel is introduced. "What need was there to recall here the name of Hur? Because he [Hur] gave up his soul for the Holy One, Blessed be He. In the hour that they sought to make the [golden] calf, he stood before them—between the people and his uncle Aaron, the high priest—and rebuked them; and they stood against him and killed him. Said the Holy One, blessed be He, to Hur: "By your life, I will compensate you for this . . . by elevating all your progeny." Thus it is written: "See, God has called Bezalel, son of Uri, son of Hur . . . and filled him with the spirit of God."

The sudden explosion of Bezalel's artistic activity is here seen as a response to the incident of the golden calf. That incident proved to the hidden, mysterious God that a spiritual life on earth was impossible without some visual, external props. To this He agreed, but on one condition that the objects act merely as a medium, valuable only insofar as they brought greater glory and praise to God. Said the invisible Creator of the Universe, recounts the midrash: "Even My own children are not prepared to recognize the truth. And if they, who saw with their own eyes all the wonders and miracles which I wrought in Egypt and in the Exodus from Egypt, do not believe, how much more so those who did not see such things!"

So God searched for someone who could distinguish between art and idolatry. He searched and He found Bezalel. Not that Bezalel was a born artist; rather, God saw his potential to serve the Divine purpose with his hands and heart and, given his lineage, could be presumed able to remain pure of idolatrous intent.

King Midas, of Greek myth, had hands whose touch turned everything to gold. Everything gold touched by Bezalel turned into something holy. Bezalel got similar results from silver, copper, ram skins, and acacia wood, as he did from stone and other materials crafted with sophisticated cutting techniques of high artistry.

The Torah's extended descriptions of the objects of the Tabernacle fill chapters of Exodus, suggesting awareness of the profound need for the aesthetic in our lives. Visual art, the Torah seems to concur, is a powerful tool. It touches the root faculty of our humanity— our imagination. It can be used to enhance or destroy us, depending on the purpose to which the artistry is put.

The medium, that is to say, is not always the message. Often the artist's technique disguises his true purpose. The objection to idolatry is not to the materials themselves—since all material has its source in God—or to their being worked into tangible images. The objection is to the assumption that material—or the image—has some intrinsic value. For idolatry is when the material presence replaces the reality it represents. This is what modern philosophers call reification, and what the Sages in their wisdom saw as a substitution of the container for the content.

LEVITICUS

A PORTABLE SINAI

Vayikra: Leviticus 1:1–5:26

Everett Fox

Of all the books of the Torah, Leviticus has the strangest and bumpiest beginning. Instead of an exalted opening, such as Genesis' "In the beginning God created the heavens and the earth," or even a straightforward one, such as Numbers' "Now the Lord spoke to Moses, saying . . . ," it begins, translated literally, "Now He called to Moses, and the Lord spoke to him . . ."

This queer syntax is hidden from the English reader by the standard translations. So, typically, the King James Version reads, "And the Lord called unto Moses, and spake unto him . . ." The more recent Jerusalem Bible has, "Yahweh called Moses, and . . . addressed him." From such as these, we would not suspect that there is anything unusual about the text.

In the Hebrew, though, the problem does not go away. Why should Leviticus, a book obsessed with order and hierarchy, begin with a sloppy sentence? The rabbis of the talmudic era sensed the difficulty with this verse, since they held that the Torah speaks in human language—and this is awkward human language indeed. Their approach was to ask why God's calling of Moses seems to be tacked in front of the more standard "The Lord spoke . . ." So, in the midrashic collection of *Vayikra Rabbah*, they used the verse for a variety of related purposes: to teach that Moses above all other Israelites deserved to be called directly by God; or that God called him specifically by the name Moses, given to him by Pharaoh's daughter; or that because of Moses' faithful execution of God's word in every detail of building the Tabernacle, he merited being called into the newly-completed Tabernacle to speak with God.

These interpretations tell us a great deal about the rabbis' veneration of Moses, but they do not solve the problem of the text. One possibility proposed by biblical scholars, following the lead of ancient translations, is that the book was once the direct continuation of Exodus, with no break. In that reading, our verse more or less directly follows a passage telling us that "the Presence of the Lord filled the Tabernacle" (Exodus 40:35), that God's "aura" came to dwell in the sanctuary people had built. Leviticus 1:1 would then simply spell out the next communication to Moses from the Divine Presence, the obvious subject of the sentence. Hence the unspecified "He" (or "It") with which the book begins.

But the fact remains that Leviticus is a separate book as we have it—so we need to look further. Now the only other biblical passage that reads "He called to Moses" comes in Exodus 24:16. We have just had several chapters of major laws, and a ceremony on Mount Sinai, in which God reveals Himself to the gathered elders of Israel, reaffirming the covenant. And then Moses is called, summoned up the mountain to receive further instruction. This instruction proves to be the architectural details of the Tabernacle. Since Leviticus 1:1 begins right after the Tabernacle's completion in Exodus

40, one could argue that in terms of literary architecture, our opening is a bracket, the second of two—setting off an important section of the Torah.

As Leviticus now stands, we might be justified in seeing its first phrase as an evocative allusion to the parallel passage in Exodus. The Sinai covenant ceremony there ended with Moses being "called" to commune further with God; and here too, we are undoubtedly meant to understand the regulations of Leviticus as stemming from God's "calling," and so as part and parcel of the Sinai experience.

The allusion in effect turns the Tabernacle into a portable Sinai of human manufacture. The Israelites can rest assured that even now, after the revelation on the mountain is past, Moses will still have the Divine word to provide them with instruction and guidance.

"Now He called to Moses: The Lord spoke to him ..." It is, in fact, a fitting beginning for a book that ends, "These are the commandments that the Lord commanded Moses for the children of Israel at Mount Sinai" (Leviticus 27:34).

STEAK AND SACRIFICES

Tzav: Leviticus 6:1–8:36

W. Gunther Plaut

Being civilized, modern people, we are likely to shudder at the idea of slicing up animals to express our devotion to God. Of course, we see nothing wrong with a good steak for dinner, unless perhaps the cardiologist advises against it. But we leave the killing of animals to others and are not inclined to improve our children's education or our own by visiting a slaughterhouse.

Yet whole chapters in the Torah are devoted to animal sacrifices; the portion of *Tzav* consists of little else. What are we to make of instructions elaborating how the animal is to be slaughtered, who may eat of it, what disposition shall be made of the fat, and who shall keep the skin? Or of the rule that the elders of the community will expiate an unwitting error made by the people through laying their hands on a bull and slaughtering it? The whole notion that the merciful Creator demands the killing of innocent creatures as a sign of human obeisance seems at first glance to be an obvious contradiction. Yet we would do well to look a little further.

First, we should consider the times and circumstances to which this legislation addressed itself. The
Israelites in the Promised Land were almost all farm-
ers, and therefore had a special relationship to their
animals and often would know them by name. They
were not accustomed to a daily diet of meat, and in that
respect were no different from the vast masses of humanity then or now. Animals were domesticated for
sale or for the milk or wool they produced. They represented capital that one did not eat up lightly.

Consuming meat was reserved for special occasions.
Chief among these were visits to the nearest shrine
and, later, to the central sanctuary in Jerusalem. These
pilgrimages were acts of festive celebration, expressed
as thanksgiving or expiation for sins committed, and
marked major events in life. The pilgrim would take
an animal along and slaughter it in the holy precincts.

As an act of worship, sacrifice had two important
side effects. For one, it served to lessen the guilt a
farmer felt (and feels) when he killed a creature he had
known from its birth. This guilt was attenuated when
the killing was done to honor God and when the meal
was shared with others. In balancing the desire to eat
meat and the moral problem of killing animals, sacrificial ritual was an extension of the wider dietary laws.
Rabbi Avraham Yitzhak Hacohen Kook, chief rabbi of
Mandatory Palestine, once wrote that all the laws of
kashrut are devised to remind us constantly that we are
eating the flesh of once-living creatures. For that reason, for instance, we do not consume animals' blood,
which in biblical tradition is considered "life itself."

Another side effect of bringing the offering in a holy
environment was the deep impression the ritual was
sure to make. This was not just killing for the sake of
pleasurable feasting; it was done for God's sake. One
came closer to God through voluntary giving of one's
possessions, through sacrificing something. (The word

"sacrifice" combines the Latin *facere*, "to make or render," and *sacer*, "holy." It is a translation of the Hebrew *korban*, "bringing close" to God.)

And we today? We buy "it" at the butcher's or in the store, probably already cellophane-wrapped. Small children have no real inkling of where the meat came from. Any connection to the living creature is totally absent. These animals are thought to have been "harvested" in some mysterious way, which even adults would rather not know about. In contrast, our biblical ancestors never reduced animals to the status of "things."

Yet we tend to feel smugly superior to those ancient times. We do so with little reason.

WHEN WORSHIP IS IDOLATRY

Shmini: Leviticus 9:1–11:47

Yeshayahu Leibowitz

On the eighth day of the festival celebrating the conse-
cration of the sanctuary and the creation of the priesthood in Israel, Aaron and his sons were consecrated
as priests. The ceremony showed that the priesthood
would be passed from father to son—something not
granted to Moses, whose sons did not inherit his role
of teaching Torah. For with the Torah, there is no continuity from generation to generation unless people
themselves create it.

Yet on that very day, Aaron's two eldest sons died in
the sanctuary, as we read in Leviticus 16:1, "when they
drew near before God [illicitly], and died." In *Shmini*,
we are given the reason for this (Leviticus 10:1): "They
presented illicit fire before God, which he did not command them." To whom did they sacrifice? To the Lord,
God of Israel, whom they wished to worship when they
"drew near before God." In no way was this compa-
rable to the worship of the golden calf. And yet, just as
many people died as a punishment for the worship of

the golden calf, as recounted in Exodus 32, in this case two of Aaron's sons died for the worship of God.

What is the meaning of the "illicit fire" that they offered before God? If we read the words as written, without any punctuation, the implication is that they did something that they were not commanded to do. Does a person deserve the death penalty simply for doing something that he was not commanded to do?

The *masorah*—the vowels and cantillation added to the biblical text in the Geonic era—offers us a certain hint: the word "not" (*lo* in the Hebrew), in the phrase "did not command," has an extremely rare cantillation sign, the *merkha kefulah*, putting a special emphasis on the word. On that basis, some of the commentators understand the sentence to mean "illicit fire which He commanded them *not* to bring." In other words, their act was not one about which they were not commanded at all, but was one that violated a specific order for them not to act as they did.

But this interpretation may be *drash*, taking us beyond the simple sense of the words, the *pshat*. And the literal meaning here may be more profound: It was possible for a person to be drawn to regard the calf as God even when his intention was, in fact, to worship God (Exodus 32:4 describes the people saying "This is your God, O Israel"—and the calf became God). And in the same way, the worship of God itself—if not performed with one's awareness that he is obeying an order of God, but because of an internal drive to serve God—is a kind of idolatry. And that is true even though the person's intentions are to serve God.

The faith that is expressed in the practical *mitzvot*, in the worship of God, is not meant to give expression or release to man's emotions. Rather, its importance lies in the fact that the person has accepted what is known in the post-biblical tradition as "the yoke of the Kingdom of Heaven and the yoke of the Torah and *mitzvot.*" Faith is expressed in the acts that man does because of his awareness of his obligation to do them, and not because of an internal urge—not even when he intends to worship God, but derives satisfaction for himself by this worship. That is illicit fire. And those who offered such fire—the first priests in the line beginning with Aaron—and did it in the sanctuary, were punished as if they had committed idolatry.

This is a very important lesson for all generations: not to transform the worship of God into a means to satisfy one's inner urges. It does not matter if one sincerely believes he is serving God; in satisfying one's own needs, one serves oneself.

A Blessing
over Differences

Tazria: Leviticus 12:1–13:59

Tzvi Marx

Debate over the religious significance of unconventional sexual identity has raged in Israel since the 1994 Supreme Court ruling that El Al must give free flights to an employee's homosexual partner, as it would to any employee's common-law spouse. As usual, attacks on accepting homosexuals have been based on the biblical proscriptions against a man "lying with a man as with a woman," deeming this "an abomination" and "punishable by death" (Leviticus 18:22 and 20:13).

Indeed, such arguments have long been used. Rabbi Moshe Tendler, for instance, has cited Leviticus [in "Extravagant Forbearance," page 247] and urged us "express shame and indignation" in response to homosexuality.

No matter how categorical scripture seems to be, though, one never assumes that a subject is closed. The classic example is the "stubborn and rebellious son" of Deuteronomy 21, to be stoned at the initiative of his parents. The Talmud, in Tractate *Sanhedrin*, creates such unlikely rules for convicting such a child that it concludes that a real one "never was and never will be."

In a matter closer to the question of sexual "deviation," the Bible excludes eunuchs from "entering the assembly of the Lord" (Deuteronomy 23:2)—that is, from marrying. Tractate *Sotah*, however, explains that the prohibition applies only to one made a eunuch by human action, but not to a congenital eunuch—apparently distinguishing between culturally chosen and physically determined deviation.

There's also a subtext of divergent rabbinic views on unconventional sexual identity in Tractate *Bekhorot*. There the Sages discuss the Torah's requirement (Exodus 34:19) that firstborn animals be consecrated unless they are physically blemished. An animal with both male and female genitals is seen by Rabbi Ishmael as having a "blemish of which none is greater." But others, as Rashi comments, consider it neither male nor female "but a creature in its own right"! In the latter view, a biological deviation is to be appreciated, not deprecated.

Defining sexual identity is made an issue in the opening verses of *Tazria*: "When a woman at childbirth bears a male, she shall be ritually impure seven days . . . and if she bears a female, she shall be impure two weeks" (Leviticus 12:2, 5). But what of a child that is both male and female, or neither (*androginus* and *tumtum* respectively in talmudic terminology)? Rather than exclude them from the law and the community because of their unusual sexual identity, the sages in Tractate *Niddah* set requirements for them between those for a male and those for a female—and so recognize such sexual identity as a category in itself.

This invites the further question, not pursued by the early sages, of how to regard a child who is conventionally male or female in some ways but not others—that is, a homosexual. While this characteristic is obviously not discernible in infancy, the long-term question is about legitimacy.

Can the Jewish community be categorical in excluding those whose differences put them outside standard sexual identity? What if those differences are a product of genes, not choice? A direction toward an answer, I suggest, can be derived from Tractate *Brakhot*, which teaches that one who sees a physically unusual person should recite: "Blessed are You, Lord, who makes creatures differently." In the thirteenth century, the Meiri—Rabbi Menahem Meir of Perpignan—explains the blessing as a response to "experiencing of new things, without necessarily enjoying or being troubled by them." What it expresses is blessed wonderment at the different forms of divinely created life.

This isn't necessarily approval. It does imply acceptance and a willingness to include in our society those destined to be different. It is consonant with the fundamental Jewish teaching that each individual is entitled to say "for me was the world created," as stated in Tractate *Sanhedrin*.

Appreciating God's creation means appreciating variations along a continuum not neatly divided. Reciting a benediction over human variety translates into creating a society in which differences are respected rather than attacked. The sacred texts, biblical or rabbinic, which appear to block such inclusion invite creative reinterpretation under the impact of new insights.

LAW OF THE LEAPER

Metzora: Leviticus 14:1–15:33

David Curzon

The ceremony belongs to a macabre Bronze Age cult. Its description begins (Leviticus 14:2): "This shall be the law of the leper in the day of his cleansing: He shall be brought unto the priest."

The priest is to look at the leper and, if the leprosy is gone, perform a number of ritual sacrifices after which the leper "shall be clean." The first ritual sacrifice involves killing one bird and dipping another in the blood of the first, and then letting the second bird go "into the open field" (Leviticus 14:7).

Even the rabbis of the Midrash, who lived much closer to the age of sacrificial rituals than we do, felt it necessary to devise techniques for avoiding the overt content of such passages and transforming them into material easier to deal with. One of the most useful of these techniques was the pun, used on the portion of *Metzora* to great effect. Don't read *metzora*, "leper," say the rabbis in *Vayikra Rabbah*, but *motzi ra*, that is, "brings forth evil." With the aid of this pun, and a few texts to prove their point, the rabbis were able to devote their sermons on our portion to the fine and relatively easy topic of the evils of gossip and slander.

It is, of course, possible to do the same with the English text. Do not read "leper" but "leaper." And this pun will in fact embody a contemporary understanding of the text. But first, following rabbinic precedent in this, too, some digression.

Is it possible to justify sacrificial rituals in contemporary terms? D.H. Lawrence did this in a poem entitled "The Old Idea of Sacrifice."

> The old idea of sacrifice was this . . .
> It was the eating up of little lives,
> even doves, even small birds
> into the dance and splendor of a bigger life.

But, of course, the slaughter of animals in sacrificial rituals no longer seems necessary to us for any purpose. Is there a rational understanding that can help us assimilate these actions of our forebears to our own sense of reason and justice? Is there some functional equivalent of the rituals described in *Metzora* that we participate in today and consider rational?

The clue to understanding the strange practices described here is that the rituals occur only after the leprosy has disappeared. The ritual is not some form of primitive medicine or exorcism that our ancestors in their ignorance thought would cure leprosy. It was a ritual designed to give a social seal of approval to an already established fact—that the disease had disappeared. The ritual was needed to reinstate the person who had been a leper as a rightful participant in community activity.

The modern analogue of all this is the graduation ceremony. The signing of a degree document must be by a person recognized as legally capable of certifying, on behalf of an institution of learning, that the student graduating is capable of practicing dentistry, law, or other acts that society allows only graduates to perform. No one thinks of the graduation ceremony itself or the certificate as creating knowledge in the previously ignorant student. But in spite of this, the act of conferring a degree is socially necessary, as anyone who has tried to get a job will testify. It is not enough to be educated, or cured. Society requires, for its proper functioning, that this be properly certified in a formal manner.

The ritual for the leper was a graduation ceremony and, like our own graduation ceremonies, marked a change in social status, a transformative leap in the lives of those certified, who jumped from social exclusion to inclusion by means of the ritual actions of a priest.

And that's why *Metzora* begins with the words "This shall be the law of the *leaper* in the day of his cleansing: He shall be brought unto the priest."

A BREAK WITH THE PAST

Aharei Mot: Leviticus 16:1–18:30

Jonathan Blass

Revolutionary progress entails the end of the status quo. "The choice and master spirits" of the age, failing to recognize that the old rules no longer apply, are often victims.

Nadab and Abihu, Aaron's two elder sons, die as the Tabernacle is dedicated, "when they drew near before the Lord" (Leviticus 16:1). The commentator Rashi writes that Moses, consoling Aaron, declares "they were greater than either of us" and that God's Name was sanctified by their deaths. Yet they were "devoured" in a fire that "went out from before the Lord," (Leviticus 10:2), punished for offering, on their own initiative, a fire "which He commanded them not."

A common thread runs through rabbinical interpretations: Nadab and Abihu wrongly stressed the spontaneous aspect of worship, preferring it to a fixed routine of Tabernacle service dictated from above. But the Tabernacle had transformed Jewish worship. Nadab and Abihu, attempting to deny the change, succeeded only in emphasizing, painfully, that it had occurred.

Until the completion of the Tabernacle, sacrifices were brought to improvised altars almost at the devotee's discretion. But the day the Tabernacle was established was compared, in Tractate *Megillah* of the Talmud, to "the day the heavens and the earth were created." The *Shekhinah*, the Divine Presence, took up permanent residence in the physical world. Now, Divine command, constant and absolute, replaced passing emotions as the basis of worship. The deaths of Nadab and Abihu, princes of the old order who were still committed to Divine service founded on human impulse, marked the line between old and new.

Aharei Mot is usually read soon after—and sometimes just before—Holocaust Day. Thus the portion, reminding us of the consequences of ignoring changes in the Jewish people and the *Shekhinah*, assumes special significance.

Like the building of the Tabernacle, the rebirth of Jewish life in the Land of Israel that began a century ago brought God and the Jewish people into a closer embrace. Like the Tabernacle, it means that an era is at an end: the Jewish renaissance in the Land of Israel augurs the Diaspora's collapse. The implication, horribly reinforced by the Holocaust, is that the mechanisms that protected the fragile life of the Diaspora can no longer be relied upon.

The continuous survival of Diaspora Jewry, unarmed and threatened by anti-Semitism and assimilation, was a miracle rivaling the Exodus from Egypt as testimony to God's intervention in history. Rabbi Shimon bar Yohai says in Tractate *Megillah*: "Wherever Israel was exiled, the Divine Presence went also." According to Tractate *Ketubot* and other sources, the laws of history were frozen to allow the existence of the Diaspora. The gentiles are described as being adjured not to oppress

Israel "unduly"—in a way that would threaten the very existence of the Diaspora—until the time of redemption. But, with the ingathering of the exiles, the Divine Presence also left exile. As the Holocaust demonstrated, the restrictions on the working of history have been lifted and the Diaspora can no longer be maintained.

The price of indulging the illusion that the past continues unaltered, the error of Nadab and Abihu, is high. The gulf between the Diaspora and Israel is a gulf between past and present, the dead and the newly resurrected. "These bones are the whole house of Israel . . . I will open your graves . . . and bring you into the Land of Israel" (Ezekiel 37: 11–12). The God of Israel has returned to His permanent address. Those remnants of His people still buried in exile must rally sufficient life-force to climb out and join Him.

NOT IN THE STARS

Kedoshim: 19:1-20:27

Micha Odenheimer

"Neither shall you practice divination or soothsaying," says Leviticus 19:26. That runs directly against an impulse as old as humanity—the desire to know what the future holds. And while the fine points of the prohibition against soothsaying are the subject of debate among halakhic authorities, as a general rule Jewish tradition prohibits the use of the stars, omens, and signs to predict the future.

We know from the Talmud that the Sages did not dismiss magical prediction as ineffective. But they believed that human beings, through their actions, could raise themselves beyond the jurisdiction of the stars. The following story, related in Tractate *Shabbat* of the Talmud, provides a good illustration of the sages' attitude toward prediction and predetermination:

> Rabbi Akiba had a daughter. The astrologers told him: "On the day she is to stand beneath the wedding canopy, a snake will bite her and she will die." Rabbi Akiba would worry about this greatly. On her wedding night, [when she let

down her hair] she took her hair pin, and stuck it into a crack
in a wall. It happened that the pin pierced the eye of a snake.
In the morning, when she pulled the pin out and put it in
her hair, the [dead] snake trailed down after her. Her father
said to her: "What did you do?" She said to him: "In the
evening, a poor man came to the door and called out, but
everyone was busy with the feast and no one heard him. I
rose, took the portion that you had served to me and gave it
to him." He said to her: "You have done a *mitzvah.*" He then
went out and preached: "'*Tzedakah* saves from death' (Proverbs 10:2) and not only from a cruel death, but from death
itself."

Etymology holds a secret here. The root of "to divine,"
in biblical Hebrew, is *NaHaSh*—which is also the word
for "snake." Akiba's daughter's act of compassion allows
her to pierce the eye of the soothsayer's snake, freeing
the future from the astrologer's destructive vision that
held it captive. In the same way, every *mitzvah* recti-
fies reality by liberating it from the death-hold that
emanates from the tree of knowledge—or the tree of
foreknowledge—where the snake lies coiled, and connecting it to the tree of life. And so: "*Tzedakah* saves
. . . from death itself."

What's more, the Torah prohibits divination not only
because the message of soothsayers sets limits on our
freedom, but because for Jews, the future itself is holy.
Rather than speak of heaven as the eventual place of
bliss and reward, Jews speak of *ha'olam haba*—the rectified world of the future. *Ha'olam haba* is usually translated as "the world to come," but a more precise translation is "the world that is coming." The promised,
perfected future is speeding toward us at the same rate,
at least, that we are rushing toward it. The future has
an existence that stands independent of whatever the
signs and omens of the present indicate. Hidden away
in inner dimensions of reality where the astrologer's
eye does not reach, the light of that future is already

shining. (On the Sabbath, "the fountain of the world to come," this light is partially revealed.)

According to Avraham Yitzhak Hacohen Kook, the great Jewish mystic and first Ashkenazi chief rabbi of Mandatory Palestine, the task of a righteous Jew is to draw the light of that rectified future into the reality of the present. "To the extent that the light of the coming world shines into this world . . ." Kook wrote, "everything is raised up . . . In order to love this world properly, one must sink oneself deeply into the love of the world to come."

The Jewish love affair with the future has the power to transform our concept of time and change our experience of the present, as Walter Benjamin, the German Jewish thinker and literary critic who died fleeing Nazi-occupied France, wrote so eloquently: "We know that the Jews were prohibited from investigating the future. . . . This does not imply, however, that for the Jews the future turned into homogeneous empty time. For every second of time was the strait gate through which the messiah might enter."

CHOICE AND LINEAGE
Emor: Leviticus 21:1–24:23

Nessa Rapoport

Can a Jew aspire to be both compassionate to all people and holy? The portion of *Emor*—mysterious, arcane, and at times terrifying—challenges the questing reader who feels mandated to emulate both these attributes of the Creator. For although it would seem essential that a holy person embody tenderness toward even the most lowly, *Emor*—whose subject is holiness—begins with exclusion and defilement and ends with deadly punishment.

These laws pertaining to the priest and high priest detail in severe, commanding language the many constraints upon the behavior of the "sons of Aaron," restrictions at whose heart are unyielding ideas of purity and profanation.

Death defiles a priest. To be worthy of offering a sacrifice, a priest cannot marry a woman who has been "defiled"—a condition that, until today, prohibits divorced or converted women from becoming wives to the descendants of Aaron. The priest must be physically unblemished as well. Blind, lame, scabbed—a long descriptive list denies access to those who are deemed to profane God's altar. In this code, holiness requires separation, and rewards distinctions based on blood lines and physical integrity rather than an earned state of righteousness.

It is curious, then, to encounter the lengthy middle section of the portion, which sets forth the holy days, from the Sabbath and Passover to Sukkot. Again, the subject is holiness; the word appears as persistently as in the rigorous opening commandments to the priests. Yet the rhetoric is utterly changed. Here are harvests, first fruits, and sweet savor. Here are feasts and rejoicing and an eternal light and covenant. And here, in the midst of such plenty, and immediately following the "peace offerings" of the harvest holiday, Shavuot, is a very different law, commanding the harvester to leave the corners of the field and the gleanings to the poor and the stranger, for "I am the Lord your God" (Leviticus 23:22).

Ah, we think, this is the compassionate God we understand, the one who weeps for his children, who recognized the stranger, Ruth—whose book we read on Shavuot—and sanctioned the purity of her chosen faith over those born into it. If we are to be, as enjoined, a kingdom of priests and a holy nation, surely it is this holiness we recognize, the one of volition and return, not that of genetic determinism?

As if to confound us symmetrically, the portion offers a coda, speaking with an austerity that corresponds to the opening passages. We read the story of a man, singled out as son of an Israelite woman and an Egyptian man, who blasphemes God. God then commands Moses to bring the man outside the camp, where all the congregation is to stone him to death.

Here, as at the start, is a list of other crimes punishable by death, of an eye for an eye, a tooth for a tooth.

And then: "You shall have one manner of law, for the stranger as for one of your own country: for I am the Lord your God" (Leviticus 24:22).

One law of holiness for priests alone. One compassionate law that favors the poor and the stranger. And one unrelenting law, for stranger and habitant alike.

Aaron and his sons could not choose to be subject to the law of the priesthood—or to escape it. But Ruth, the poorest stranger, a Moabite convert retrieving the harvest gleanings, could choose the law that then sanctioned her as a fitting ancestor of King David and of the redeemer.

Let us choose between the mode of Aaron and the mode of Ruth as scrupulously as these modes of law are delineated in *Emor*. And let us note the paradox implicit in several kinds of law set forth as one: when we embrace the excluding code of priesthood, remember that Ruth came from an alien land and people. And when we stone the blasphemer—half-Israelite, half-Egyptian—outside the camp, recall his blood lineage and remember this: his mother's name was Shlomit (Leviticus 24:11)—wholeness, peace.

Caretakers on God's Estate

Behar: Leviticus 25:1–26:2

Harold M. Schulweis

One of the contemporary distortions of the biblical ethos comes from some spokesmen of the ecological movement. The gravamen is based on the biblical mandate to "subdue" the earth and "have dominion over the fish of the sea, and over the fowl of the air and over every living thing that moves on the earth" (Genesis 1:28). This verse is taken to warrant the exploitation of nature. The Bible's "disenchantment of nature," as sociologist Max Weber described it, is claimed to have encouraged science and technology to rape the earth.

The roots of the critique go back at least to nineteenth-century philosopher Ludwig Feuerbach, who attacked Judaism in his "The Essence of Christianity" for its egoistic doctrine of creation. "The Israelites . . . [opened] to nature only the gastric sense. Their taste of nature lay only in the palate."

It is true that the Bible's religious humanism regards the human being as the crown of creation. But that in no way implies the denigration of nature. This por-

tion, *Behar*, includes key evidence of the dignity of
the earth. The earth breathes, labors, and requires
rest. Resources are not to be squeezed out of the earth
on the seventh day (Leviticus 25:3–6), and the land
requires a "sabbath of the Lord" in the seventh year
(Leviticus 25:4). The sabbath of the land expresses a
covenant between humankind and nature.

Nor is such concern for creation restricted to *Behar*.
Towards the animal world, there are reiterated passages of concern. Animals, Maimonides reminds us
in the *Guide for the Perplexed*, may not be endowed
with the cognitive powers of human beings, but they
have feelings like our own which must be respected.
This empathic approach is rooted in dozens of Biblical laws, such as Deuteronomy 22:4: "If you see your
fellow's ass or ox fallen on the road, do not ignore it
. . ." This attitude informs Jewish law to the extent that
shouting at an animal to frighten it away from eating
from the fields it works is prohibited by the *Shulhan
Arukh* (in *Hoshen Hamishpat*): "Men may be forbidden to consume that which they harvest, but animals
must be allowed to eat if they desire, for while man
can understand deprivations, animals cannot."

How men with whips, rods, traps, and swords deal
with dumb, dependent, and helpless creatures conditions the way they treat the weak of the human species.
There is a moral correlation between the prohibition on
muzzling the ox when he treads out the corn, denying
it the opportunity to graze (Deuteronomy 25:4), and the
injunction to allow a man to eat grapes in his neighbor's
vineyard to his heart's content (Deuteronomy 23:25).
Though a man can exercise restraint, the text is sensi-
tive to the temptations of human nature.

The compassion towards the feeling and life of sentient creatures moves us closer to the vegetarian ideal
of Eden, where human beings were given only "every
seed-bearing plant . . . and every tree that has seed-

bearing fruit . . . for food" (Genesis 1:29), and to the messianic vision of the carnivorous beasts becoming herbivores, when "the lion shall eat straw like the ox" (Isaiah 11:7). In the last days, as in the first, the life of sentient creatures will not be taken.

Rabbinic tradition explicitly declared that consideration for the pain caused animals is biblical law *("Tza'ar ba'alei hayyim de'oraita"*—Tractate *Bava Metzia)*. The mode of slaughtering animals was designed to cause the animal the least possible pain. The blade of the knife must be sharp as a razor, the two strokes of the knife must be rapid in continuous motion, back and forward without even a moment's delay.

The earth is lent to human beings, but not as if they were lords of the land, but as stewards of the Lord's estate. Precisely because the "earth is the Lord's," people may not do with it as they wish. "The land is not to be sold in perpetuity" (Leviticus 25:23). The surrender of ownership to God places restraints upon the use and exploitation of the earth. The biblical prohibition against destroying any fruit trees in conducting military operations (Deuteronomy 20:19) was expanded by the rabbis into a general prohibition against wanton destruction *(bal tash'hit).*

Central to *Behar* is the Jubilee, the fiftieth year in which the slaves and their families are emancipated and property restored to its original owners (Leviticus 25:8-19). The Jubilee is a cosmic year of *teshuvah*— a return to the harmony and wholeness of creation. Slaves are freed and property reverts to its owners on a Day of Atonement for all creation. Cosmic *teshuvah* includes the repair of individual men and women, society as a whole, and the land itself. The Jubilee return dramatizes the interdependence of creation and, as Leviticus 25:10 states, "proclaims liberty throughout the land unto all the inhabitants thereof."

AN END TO CHAOS

Behukkotai: Leviticus 26:3–27:34

Shulamith Hareven

Like much of Leviticus, *Behukkotai* may sound disso-
nant to the modern reader. The laws—and the consequences of observing or violating them, spelled out in
such detail—are not a democratic constitution, reached
after long deliberation by a legislative body. The Divine
Persona is intimidating and peremptory. There are no
questions, and the only answer seems to be the blunt
repetition, "I am the Lord,"—that is, "because I say so."

But the essence of what was given at the encamp-
ment near Mount Sinai is normativism. This is no
longer the capricious world of polytheism and idolatry, where man's fate is unpredictable because gods
disagree. Nor is it the always-unpredictable world of
slavery. Chaos ends. In this code of law, there is clear
differentiation between good and bad behavior, not
random but absolute, and with it the assurance of inex-
orable reward and punishment.

The Divine Persona says to the people who have just
left Egypt, where the only consistency was the lack of

it: From now on, your behavior, not the whim of gods
or slave drivers, will determine your fate. By accepting a code of law, you become responsible for what you
do and the result will not be a matter of luck. It may
be a harsh law, but there will be no surprises.

To the men and women at Sinai, this must have been
revolutionary. For the first time, what they do matters.
There is a possibility of choice, even if to the modern
reader it is hardly a real personal choice. Moreover, the
code of law in Leviticus is as binding for God as for the
people. This is a written text, a contract bearing God's
own signature—"I am the Lord."

Change the authority of God to the authority of state,
and you are close to modern perceptions. This is the
social contract between citizen and state, except that
nowadays we do not mobilize bad weather, war, and
plagues. A good citizen may count on being defended;
lawbreakers will be punished.

And there is no hereafter (how strange this must
have sounded after Egypt!), no promise of resurrec-
tion or a messianic era. Any reward or punishment
will be here and now. The Divine Persona is no more
concerned with the hereafter than a modern judiciary
would be. Christianity's emphasis on faith and promise of paradise and hell sounds almost regressive compared to the realistic premise of these statutes, concerned not with personal faith, but with personal
responsibility.

Notice the mood of the Lawgiver: the whole tone is
one of a great hurry. Threats are used when there is
no time to convince. Perhaps we can discern an underlying anxiety to convey the essentials. Perhaps there
is also anger, an expression of the pain of betrayal, not
so long ago, in this very spot. After the golden calf, the
sentence: "These are the statutes and judgments and
laws which the Lord made between Him and the children of Israel at Mount Sinai by the hand of Moses," is

a sad one. You have transgressed, you have betrayed,
but life must go on and we must agree on a code of law
to ensure that it does—in this place, while we are still
here—never mind the pain, which I still feel and choose
to overlook.

And there is love. "And yet for all that . . . I will not
cast them away, neither will I abhor them, to destroy
them utterly."

True, *Behukkotai* is intimidating. It is rigid, imposed,
terse, clerical, not very appealing to the modern mind.
Still, the norms of mainstream halakhic Judaism are
all there: personal responsibility, equality before the
law, even for the stranger in our midst, little concern
with faith, and not much patience with the hereafter.
Not a bad beginning.

NUMBERS

TO THE WILDERNESS
Bemidbar: Numbers 1:1–4:20

Micha Odenheimer

Revelation came in the wilderness, the first sentence of the Book of Numbers stresses: "And God spoke to Moses in the wilderness of Sinai, from the Tent of Meeting . . ." And, says the midrash in *Bemidbar Rabbah*, wilderness is a necessary condition for every revelation, for every true internalization of the Torah's teaching: "Whoever would wish to acquire Torah, must make himself ownerless like the wilderness."

What does it mean to be ownerless? Why wilderness?

For Maimonides, writing in the twelfth century, wilderness represents the means of escaping the seductive influence of an evil society, an influence powerful enough to "own" you. "If all the countries he knows or hears of follow evil ways, as is the case in our time," he says in his *Mishneh Torah*, then one must "go out into the caves, the clefts of mountains, and the wilderness" to save himself from a degenerate society's mores.

Rabbi Nahman of Bratslav, six centuries later, also contrasts the sanctuary offered by wilderness to so-

ciety's corruption. But in his depiction, in the story
"The Master of Prayer," societies have sunk one step
below evil—into insanity. The story describes a series
of countries, each organized around its own mad obsession. In one, money is worshiped so totally that it
has become the key to human identity: "Whoever had
more money was a human being, and those who were
very wealthy were considered gods." The master of
prayer subversively penetrates these societies and
draws people "out of the settled places," into the wilderness and a life of prayer and meditation.

Prayer is the antidote to society's obsessions because
it alone has the power to lift consciousness out of the
web of socially conditioned desires into a new matrix
whose center is God. Prayer, the effort to reach out—
and in—toward the transcendent, to stand before the
One, creates a wilderness within, where a person can
be alone with God. Even during public prayer, the cre-
scendo of intensity is reached during the whispered
amidah, whose sound should not be heard by another
human being.

To become a master of prayer involves breaking,
at least for a few precious moments, the norms for
"proper" behavior, whose first principle is the constant, vigilant awareness of oneself as a social animal.
The following scene from the nineteenth-century hasidic work *Abir Haro'im*—like descriptions of prayer
from biblical times to today—shares this characteristic of wilderness:

> Rabbi Avigdor Yehudah Halevy, the rabbi of Koy, used to
> remain the whole day, until night fell, in the synagogue,
> with the doors locked . . . It happened once that . . . people
> looked in the windows . . . He was lying on the floor in *tallit*
> and *tefillin*, stretched out, arms and legs extended in full
> prostration before the Holy Ark, which was open, and sur-
> rounding his holy body were many white doves. And so was
> he pouring out his heart in prayer before his Creator, Blessed
> be He."

Perhaps no civilization has been as aware as ours of the extent to which identity and consciousness are conditioned—by history, social class, economics, biology. After Marx, Darwin, Freud, Nietzsche, Foucalt, and Derrida, we see human consciousness as lacking a center, identity as false, language as "an infinite play of reference" with no meaning outside itself.

And as forests and deserts have disappeared from most of our lives, so has prayer. Or rather, it has been repressed, as sexuality was repressed in previous generations and heresies in still earlier ones. People may still pray, but prayer—wild, heart-rending prayer—is almost never represented in mainstream culture. You don't hear it on the radio or see it on TV, in movies or in literary creations. If you do it is seen as slightly shameful or embarrassing, or as reflecting despair or even madness.

Yet we need prayer. We need to ground our identity in the hope of the absolute. Only through prayer can we "acquire the Torah," find meaning in language, receive transmitted truth.

And, as Freud taught us, the repressed has a way of returning in grotesque, horrific forms. It returns in the Muslim shouting *Allahu akbar* while detonating a car bomb, in the Jew who rises for his sunrise prayer only to train his gun on human beings kneeling in devotion.

We have driven prayer into the fringes. We must learn to pray for peace with abandon if we are to steal prayer back from violence.

WAR DAMAGE

Naso: Numbers 4:21–7:89

Micha Odenheimer

Who fought the first religious war? The answer, according to Genesis, is Cain and Abel: "Cain brought an offering to the Lord from the fruit of the soil; and Abel, for his part, brought the choicest of the firstlings of his flock. The Lord paid heed to Abel and his offering, but to Cain and his offering He paid no heed. Cain was much distressed and his face fell . . . And the Lord said: 'Why has your face fallen . . . Surely, if you do right, there is uplift . . .' And when they were in the field, Cain set upon his brother and killed him. Then [the Lord] said: 'You shall be cursed.'"

The midrash, in *Breshit Rabbah*, brings this first war into the context of Jewish history by connecting it to the Temple. What were Cain and Abel actually fighting over? Rabbi Yehoshua of Sakhnin says, in the name of Rabbi Levi: "Over whose land the Temple would be built on. How do we know this? For it says, 'And when they were in the field,' and field refers to the Temple, as it says, 'And Zion will be plowed under like a field.'"

145

In the Torah itself, the original trauma of the first murder seems, after having been duly described in the narrative, to disappear without a trace. But if we remain open to the hint provided by Rabbi Yitzhak Luria, the renowned seventeenth-century kabbalist, we may discover a response to the story at the center of the Torah—literally. Rabbi Luria teaches that the relationship between Aaron and Moses, the brothers who led the children of Israel out of Egypt, is a *tikkun*—a repair—of the damage to reality caused by Abel's murder.

With this, look at the passage that, if you count the verses, comes in the exact middle of the Torah—Leviticus 8:8. It describes the moment when Moses placed the jeweled breastplate of the high priest on Aaron's chest, initiating his brother into his priestly role. That action is symbolic of the mutual love and acceptance of each other's role that defined the brothers' relationship. Rashi connects this passage with Exodus 4:14, which describes Aaron coming to greet Moses "with joy in his heart"—the opposite of Cain's jealousy—after having learned of his younger brother's election by God as Israel's redeemer from Egypt. "From this joy," the midrash says, "Aaron merited the bejeweled breastplate that is placed over his heart," and, one might add, the priesthood itself.

The charge—and the method—of repairing the damage rendered by Cain is passed on to Aaron's children. In *Naso*, the priests are commanded to bless the children of Israel. This must be done "with love," the Talmud dictates in Tractate *Sotah*—the blessing must come from the heart. In addition, the Talmud says in the same tractate, any priest who has ever killed a man, even by accident, may not bless the people.

The text of the blessing in Numbers 6:22–27, when examined closely, alludes to the major movements in the Cain and Abel narrative, though in reverse order, for the priests must begin the "repair" from the lowest point the brothers reached. The first of the blessings, "The Lord bless you and keep you," is, on the simple level, a "repair" of the human vulnerability of which Abel is archetype. But it also counters Cain's infamous dismissal of responsibility, "Am I my brother's keeper?" Cain's feeling of humiliation—"His face fell," which the *Tikkunei Zohar* explains as a sudden reduction of the Divine light that should radiate from the human face, is healed with the blessing, "The Lord make His face shine upon you." And the final blessing, "The Lord lift up His countenance to you and grant you peace," refers both to what God had promised Cain if he would overcome his anger and sadness—"there will be uplift"—and to what Cain had desired in the first place, that God turn to him and acknowledge his sacrifice.

From the blessings, we see that all of us need a "repair"—not only of the vulnerability that Abel's murder implies about men, but of the humiliation and rejection that Cain felt, for both these possibilities exist in all of us. And although God cursed Cain, the healing must come through a blessing delivered by our fellow man. Such is the implication of the verses that preface and follow the blessing: Only after the commandment is fulfilled to "place My name upon the children of Israel," can God say, "and I will bless them."

HUMILITY OF A PROPHET

Beha'alotkha: Numbers 8:1–12:16

Yeshayahu Leibowitz

The portion of *Beha'alotkha* includes the story (which we do not understand completely) of a dispute between Miriam and Aaron and their brother Moses, and here we find a comment that "the man Moses was very humble, more than any man on earth" (Numbers 12:3). Many earlier and later rabbinic commentators have noted that from the deeds of Moses, we already know much of him by this point in the Torah—that he is the redeemer of Israel, its legislator, the performer of miracles and wonders—and we have come to appreciate his personality. But the Torah does not specifically describe his character, except for this one place where it specifically notes one of his qualities.

Nowhere does the Torah state explicitly that Moses was wiser, or more righteous, or heroic, than any man, although we can deduce from the events that he was wise, with great insight, and that he was righteous and heroic. But the Torah finds it proper, or necessary, to stress only one thing: that he was more humble than any other man.

This gives us food for thought. Humility is a high level of human character. Human nature is such that most ordinary persons consider themselves—if not consciously, at least subconsciously—to be worthy and important. It is not natural for a person to be humble. The humbleness sometimes found among some people of a high status or a high intellectual and ethical character can be the product of one of two factors: either they, through self-criticism, are aware of their faults or weaknesses; or they have overcome man's nature of venerating himself, boasting, and praising himself, and act modestly and appear as humble.

In which way was Moses "humble"? He was the man who attained the highest comprehension of God that man is able to attain. One might then imagine that for a person who had reached that high a level, it would be psychologically impossible not to be conscious of his superiority. We even find one of the great prophets in Israel, many centuries after Moses, warning—at God's command—that no man should boast of his wisdom, his might or his wealth, but explicitly allowing a man "to boast of this, that he understands and knows Me, that I am God" (Jeremiah 9:22). Yet Moses attained a comprehension of God which was superior to that of any of the prophets. The Talmud states in Tractate *Yevamot*: "All the prophets looked [on God] through a murky glass; our master Moses looked [on Him] through a clear glass."

Precisely from this we should learn that only he who really "understands and knows" is able to realize that man cannot understand and know God, and thus acquires the truest and deepest humility.

If the perception of the prophet tells him that he apprehends God—he has reason to exult. But Moses— of whom we are told that God spoke to him "face to face" (Exodus 33:11) and that "he is trusted through-out My household" (Numbers 12:7), and "that God knew him face to face" (Deuteronomy 34:10)—under-stands that God is beyond human comprehension.

To this highest level of humbleness in the relation-ship of man to God, the great medieval commen-tator Rashi gives a formulation by adding to the above-mentioned talmudic statement a few keen words: "All the prophets looked through a murky glass—and thought that they saw; our master Moses looked through a clear glass—and knew that he had not seen Him to His face."

THE FACTS, JUST THE FACTS

Shlah Lekha: Numbers 13:1–15:41

Hillel Halkin

It might be asked why the ten spies who returned from Canaan with the recommendation to cancel Operation Promised Land are treated so harshly by the Bible. They were sent on an information-gathering mission, and by all accounts they performed it well. "Go see what the land is," said Moses, and they went and reported what they saw: The land was rich and flowed with milk and honey. "And see whether the people who dwell in it are strong or weak," he briefed them, and they did: The people in the land were tall and strong. "And see whether the cities they dwell in are undefended or fortified," they were ordered, and they told the truth this time too: The cities were fortified and large. Were they supposed to have lied to suit Moses' plans? But in that case, what was the point of sending them in the first place? As we Israelis learned the hard way in the Yom Kippur War, it is a poor intelligence service that is prepared to hear only good news.

The ten spies came back with the facts. The biblical story does not dispute this. What did they do that was wrong?

"The Amalekites dwell in the land of the Negev; the Hittites, the Jebusites, and the Amorites dwell in the hill country; and the Canaanites dwell by the sea, and along the Jordan," the ten sum up, professionally, leaving the decision-making to others. On the heels of which, the next verse tells us: "But Caleb quieted the people before Moses and said: 'Let us go up at once, and occupy it [the land], for we are well able to overcome it.'" Clearly, the biblical narrative has skipped something here, and what it has skipped is clear, too: it is the people's reaction to the ten spies' account. Indeed, the voices quieted by Caleb are obviously the same ones that we hear of a few verses further on when we read: "Then all the congregation raised a loud cry [and said]: 'Why does the Lord bring us into this land— to fall by the sword? Would it not be better for us to go back to Egypt?'"

But of course, if neither going back to Egypt nor remaining marooned in the desert is a viable option, a practical consideration that the spies do not seem to think should have been any of their business in formulating their report, there is no realistic choice but to press ahead. And so even if the odds are not the best, Caleb—who along with Joshua has brought back a dissenting opinion—tries arguing for Canaan.

The ten spies disagree with such demagoguery and feel conscience-bound to abandon their neutrality: "We are not able to go up against the people [of Canaan]; for they are stronger than we." And yet, even at this point, it can be claimed that they are only doing their duty, which is to give their honest appraisal of the situation, and even at this point, the Bible voices no criticism of them. It is only in the following verse that we are told: "So they brought to the people of Israel an evil report of the land which they had spied out, saying: 'The land, through which we have gone, to spy it out, is a land that devours its inhabitants . . . and we seemed to ourselves like grasshoppers, and so we seemed to them.'"

Now obviously a land that flows with milk and honey is not a land that devours its inhabitants, nor are the proportions of an Israelite to even a very tall Canaanite those of an insect to a man. What has happened here is that the spies, realizing that like it or not they have a responsibility to mold public opinion, have for the first time been tempted to . . . Well, let us not say that they lied or exaggerated; let us say that they failed to check their notes. The people panic, God loses His temper, and the rest is biblical history.

Or would be if it did not sound so familiar. What did you say was the profession that has been accused of bringing an evil report of Israel, although it is only fair to point out in its defense that it is merely giving us the facts?

KORAH AMONG US

Korah: Numbers 16:1–18:32

Yeshayahu Leibowitz

Korah follows the Torah portion of *Shlah Lekha*, whose last verses deal with *tzitzit*. Those verses also make up the last section of the *Shema*. It would appear that there is no link between the end of *Shlah Lekha* and the beginning of *Korah*. Yet they are closely linked by a key word that appears in both.

The section on *tzitzit* concludes: "That you may remember, and do all my *mitzvot*, and *be holy* to your God: I am your God." Immediately after this, we read: "Korah, the son of Izhar . . . and Dathan and Abiram, the sons of Eliab, and On, son of Peleth . . . and 250 notable Israelites" rebelled against Moses and Aaron, claiming: "All the community [of Israel], all of them *are holy*, and God is among them all; why do you lift yourselves above them?"

Thus we have the term "holy" twice. But the difference between the holiness mentioned in the verses on *tzitzit* and that expressed by *Korah* is the difference between faith in God and idolatry. The holiness connected with *tzitzit* is not a fact, but a goal. We are not told, "You are holy." Rather, there is a demand—a demand that it is doubtful any person can meet, but one that each person must be aware is demanded of him: You are to be holy. In Korah's view, holiness is something granted to us: We are holy.

In the verses on *tzitzit*, holiness is expressed as the most lofty state man can attain by cleaving to God and his Torah, and he is required to demand this goal of himself. And the believer sees this task as a great privilege given him. On the other hand, Korah and his adherents have a cheap notion of holiness: the person absolves himself of responsibility, of the task imposed upon him and of the obligation to exert himself; he is smugly sure that he is already holy. Even the most contemptible person can boast of belonging to a holy nation.

In the long history of Judaism, these two concepts of holiness have existed side by side. From one of them, the entire world of halakhah developed. Its laws are the expression of the striving of man to be near to God by directing his behavior according to what he sees as obligations imposed on him in accordance with the Torah. But there were and are believers in a holiness which is inherent in the Jewish people, and above the performance or non-performance of obligations. We are told that Korah and his followers were swallowed up by the earth, but that his sons did not die. Korahites exist to this very day, whose religious faith is the reliance on the holiness granted to the Jewish people and who feel that they are already at the level which man is ordered in the *Shma* to eternally attempt to attain.

A contemporary religious thinker, Rabbi Ya'akov Moshe Harlap, formulated the issue marvelously, in a commentary on Maimonides' *Eight Chapters*: What is the most important thing in man's reality? (And for Rabbi Harlap, "man's reality" is, of course, his standing before God.) Is it what man achieves, or the efforts that go into achieving it? He concludes that it is the efforts, whose value is independent of whether the goal is achieved and even if the goal is achievable. It is possible that the condition that the Torah makes for man's being holy, "That you may remember and do all my *mitzvot*" is beyond human nature, but man is nevertheless commanded to attempt to fulfill it, to attempt to be holy.

But the Korahite view of a holiness implicit in the Jewish people is also held by some great believers. It is found in the religious thought of Rabbi Yehudah Halevi (in his *The Kuzari*) and of the Maharal of Prague, and closer to our generation, in the thought of Rabbi Avraham Yitzhak Hacohen Kook. Kook forgot the importance of "separating between holy and profane," and sought and found holiness in the very existence of the Jewish people, and thereby led astray his disciples and the disciples of his disciples, both spiritually and in their actions.

There is a vast difference between the holiness of the end of the *Shma* and holiness as understood by Korah and his cohorts, who were evidently not swallowed up by the ground, and still live to this very day.

GOD IS NO DICTATOR

Hukkat: Numbers 19:1–22:1

Reuven Hammer

In his comments on the Torah reading of Shmini ("When Worship Is Idolatry," page 107), Yeshayahu Leibowitz restated his well-known position that "The faith that is expressed in the practical *mitzvot*, in the worship of God, is not meant to give expression or release to man's emotions." He goes so far as to say that even one who "intends to worship God, but derives satisfaction for himself from this worship . . . is [offering] illicit fire."

True, awareness of serving God is an important part of the system of *mitzvot*. Yet is performance of *mitzvot* to fulfill human needs to be totally rejected? All ritual has a certain arbitrariness. But there is a tension within Judaism between the arbitrary and the meaningful, between Divine fiat and human needs.

The law of the red heifer (Numbers 19:1–10) serves as an excellent example. The ashes of a heifer, all of whose hairs were red, are mixed with water, then sprinkled on people who have become impure through contact with the dead, in order to render them pure. Yet the man who burns the heifer becomes impure.

This ritual appears completely arbitrary, to be performed only because God has ordered it. And that feeling may be strengthened by an account in *Bemidbar Rabbah*: A pagan challenged Rabban Yohanan ben Zakkai, saying: "This rite [of the red heifer] . . . appears to be a kind of sorcery." The sage responded by comparing the ritual with the exorcising of madness. The individual, he explained, has been "possessed" by the spirit of impurity, which must be exorcised. When his students protested afterwards that this was a poor answer, he said: "In truth, the corpse does not defile, nor do the ashes and the water have the power to purify. Rather the Holy One says, 'I have made a statute, I have decreed a decree. You are not permitted to transgress My decree.'"

Yet only two paragraphs earlier in the same midrash, we are told that the Holy One said to Moses, "Unto you I reveal the meaning of the commandment of the red heifer. For others, it is a decree." It goes on to say, "Those matters that are hidden in this world will be revealed in the world to come." The rabbis were not willing to admit that even this command was without purpose. What's more, the same midrashic text overflows with attempts to confer meaning on obscure commandments. For example, it explains why certain plants are used in rites of purifying the leper—the cedar because he was smitten as punishment for haughtiness; the hyssop because now that he is humble, he can be cured (Leviticus 14). The Torah explicitly takes human feelings into account when it ordains that certain offerings be brought when we have sinned and wish to make atonement or when we want to express thanksgiving to God.

If we look at its origins, we find that the law of the red heifer was indeed intended to speak to human needs. As Jacob Milgrom points out in his commentary to Numbers, modern study of ancient Near Eastern religion has helped us to understand matters once obscure. In paganism, the impurity of death assumed mythological proportions. The fear of such contamination was deep-seated in human beings—as, in fact, it still is. Paganism responded with magic rites that helped the forces of purity overcome the forces of impurity. In the Torah, none of that mythic conflict remains. The color red, the color of blood that symbolizes life, is invoked ceremonially to overcome impurity. But there are no magic formulas, only the power of God. It is He who purifies, as indicated by Jeremiah (17:13) who, in a play on words, called God the "*mikveh* of Israel"—the Hebrew term meaning both "hope" and "purifying bath."

In asserting that "the ashes and the water do not have the power to purify," Rabban Yohanan ben Zakkai was only reaffirming this rejection of paganism's magic. He was not denying the role of ritual in helping us to cope with crises we all face.

God is not a dictator who orders us around simply to demonstrate that He can do so. We picture Him rather as "Our Father, our King." A king commands obedience, but a father loves His children. He wants to meet their needs. The more we can perform *mitzvot* that we understand, that answer our needs, and that help us to be more fully human, the closer we are to fulfilling the Divine will.

With Blessings Like This

Balak: Numbers 22:2–25:9

Hillel Halkin

So Balak the son of Zippor, who was king of Moab, sent
messengers to Balaam the son of Beor ... saying: "Behold, a
people has come out of Egypt; they cover the face of the
earth, and they are dwelling opposite me. Come now, curse
this people for me, since they are too mighty for me; perhaps I shall be able to defeat them and drive them from the
land; for I know that he whom you bless is blessed, and he
whom you curse is cursed." (Numbers 22: 4–6)

It is indeed a charming story, complete with a talk-
ing donkey, an invisible angel, the ritual repetitions
of folktale, and no small amount of comedy, since each
time the trusting Balak gets his expectations back
up that at long last the slippery Balaam will put the
whammy on Israel, oops!—out comes another blessing
instead of a curse. "For I know that he whom you bless
is blessed, and he whom you curse is cursed"—and
so the word comes from God to Balaam, and Balaam
blesses Israel, and Israel, in an ironic reversal of its
enemy's intentions, is blessed.

Are we really?

"How can I curse whom God has not cursed? How can I denounce whom the Lord has not denounced? For from the top of the mountains I see him, from the hills I behold him; lo, a people dwelling alone, and not reckoning itself among the nations!" (Numbers 23:8-9)

A people dwelling alone and not reckoning itself among the nations. If that is a blessing, perhaps we should have been cursed.

Perhaps we were. The fact is that philo-Semites like Balaam have always made me nervous. The line separating a philo- from an anti- is not even as wide as the hyphen after each. Anti-Semitism is a complicated matter. I wouldn't go so far as to say that we've deserved it. But a people dwelling alone and not reckoning itself among the nations is not going to be liked. Admired—certainly. Even in ancient times, there were people who admired us. Resented—of course. Jew-resentment is considerably older than Christianity. But liked? As much as you liked the boy at school who sat in the corner reading during recess when everyone else was playing punchball in the yard and who gave you a superior look when you trooped back into the classroom.

The Bible is a very subtle book. Look for the unstated connections. "Then Balaam rose, and went back to his place; and Balak also went his way." But read on. "And Israel dwelt in Shittim, and the people began to whore with the daughters of Moab . . . And behold, one of the people of Israel came and brought a Midianite woman to his family, in the sight of Moses and in the sight of the whole congregation of the people of Israel . . . And when Pinhas the son of Eleazar, son of Aaron the priest, saw it, he rose and left the congregation, and took a spear in his hand and went after the man of Israel into the inner room, and pierced both of them, the man of Israel and the woman, through her vagina . . .

And those that died in the plague [inflicted in punishment by God for reckoning themselves among the nations] were twenty-four thousand" (Numbers 25:1–9).

In Jewish tradition, Pinhas is a hero. I do not know what he is in Midianite tradition, but it is not hard to guess.

"For I know that he whom you bless is blessed, and he whom you curse is cursed."

As I said, an ironic chapter.

AN ANGRY YOUNG MAN

Pinhas: Numbers 25:10–30:1

Gershom Gorenberg

The story is built around age: An older man, Moses, and an angry young one, Pinhas, confront each other on a desert plain, and the young one takes the law into his own hands. How you read the story is also a matter of age. If you don't side with Pinhas when you're twenty, you have no spirit. If you still side with him years later, I've begun to suspect, you have no sense.

To sketch the scene: The Israelites are camped in the plains of Moab. It's been nearly forty years since the revolution in Egypt, and since a new order was proclaimed at Sinai. And here, so close to Canaan they can smell the promise of its fields, whole crowds of Israelites are seduced, literally and theologically, by local Moabite and Midianite women, and follow them to feast before their idol. God is incensed, and Moses tells the courts of law to pass death sentences for treason. But law has crumbled: one Zimri, a ringleader of the tribe of Simeon, pulls a Midianite noblewoman to the center of the camp and into his tent, while Moses and the people watch and impotently weep. The new order is collapsing, and courts and judges move too slowly to save it.

It's then the young priest Pinhas, of the tribe of Levi, rises, strides to the tent, and thrusts his spear through the copulating couple. The revolution is saved, and God rewards Pinhas's impulsive passion by reaffirming his hereditary right to the high priesthood.

So I once read the Torah's brief synopsis. And it's worth adding two dialogues: one, from a medieval midrash called *Pitaron Hatorah*, portrays Zimri holding the woman's hand and confronting Moses. "What's the law on her?" he asks.

"Forbidden, like all Midianites," says Moses.

"And what about your wife Zipporah the Midianite?"

"I married her before the Torah was given, and anyway I converted her."

"What you guys want," says Zimri, apparently an angry young man himself, "you always justify," and Moses is speechless.

Zimri, in fact, is a mirror image of Pinhas, headstrong, certain he knows better than the law. So I imagine a second dialogue moments later.

"What court ordered you to execute him?" Moses demands of Pinhas.

"What court told you to kill the slavemaster in Egypt?"

"That," the old man answers, "was before the Torah, and anyway, what Egyptian court would have protected us?"

"What you guys want, you always justify," says Pinhas; and a voice from heaven, promising him "a covenant of eternal priesthood" (Numbers 25:12) shows whose side God is on.

Or so I used to see it, but I find the nuances shifting.

Watching Zimri and womanfriend saunter into their tent, the Moses who once slew a slavemaster knows about the option of the spear. He also sees the gash that zealotry can cut in the order he's spent a life building, based on judges, rules of evidence, and deliberation, not on revolutionary justice. He senses the precedent an action like Pinhas's will set—particularly for angry men who confuse hatred of anyone foreign with virtue, or who suppress the passion Zimri feels by turning it into violence against sinners. Yet Moses knows his camp is turning into chaos. There aren't easy answers, and he cries.

Those dialogues—or rather Moses's silences at their end—also sound different now. Zimri and Pinhas want him to be consistent; he wants to say, Listen, sometimes consistency is the most foolish of vices. Pinhas wants him to defend principle; he wants to reply, Sometimes principles clash. He isn't the last parent or leader to go silent in such moments, nor the first: his great-great-grandfather Jacob asked Simeon and Levi, the ancestors and antetypes of Zimri and Pinhas, why they'd murdered every man in Shechem to revenge a rape; when they answered, "Should our sister be treated as a whore?" (Genesis 34:31), he realized there are times when age and youth share no language.

But what of God's verdict, the "covenant of everlasting priesthood"? I'm not sure. But perhaps as Moses sat in his tent that night, he mused that there is no role in the Torah as defined by rules and protocol as the high priesthood. In return for the holy position, the high priest surrenders all room for impulse or passion—and Pinhas, Moses could comfort himself, had been co-opted into a lifetime of penance.

WHERE THE LIVING IS EASY

Matot: Numbers 30:2–32:42

Reuven Hammer

We may be the only people to have created a Diaspora before settling a homeland. The tribes of Reuben and Gad asked Moses to permit them to stay on the east bank of the Jordan rather than crossing into the land of milk and honey and occupying the territory they had been assigned there: "The Reubenites and the Gadites owned cattle in very great numbers ... 'The land that the Lord has conquered for the community of Israel is cattle country, and your servants have cattle ... We will build here sheepfolds for our flocks and towns for our children ...'" (Numbers 32).

The rabbis understood well the motivation of these tribes. As the midrash states in *Bemidbar Rabbah*:

> The Gadites and the Reubenites were wealthy and had much cattle. They prized their money and therefore settled outside the Land of Israel. Therefore, they were sent into captivity and exile [by the Assyrians] before the other tribes ... They made trivial things important, and made the important trivial, for they valued money more than people, for

173

they said to Moses: "We will build here sheepfolds for our flocks," and only then "and towns for our children" (Numbers 32:16). Moses said to them, "First things first! 'Build towns for your children' and then 'sheepfolds for your flocks' (Numbers 32:24).

To desire to live in a place of wealth and comfort even at the expense of other values is normal. Hordes of Jews seeking a good life a hundred years ago, my grandparents included, left Russia not for the land of milk and honey, but for the Golden Land, as America was known in Yiddish. Today, a new Diaspora of former Israelis is made up largely of those who felt that a better living was to be had in America than in Israel. Perhaps they were right. Hopefully, they will at least put their children before their cattle and give them a good Jewish education, lest they assimilate even more quickly than other American Jews.

The tribes of Reuben and Gad also faced the problem of retaining Jewish identity in the Diaspora. They erected a "great conspicuous altar" (Joshua 22:10) by the Jordan. The other tribes thought that they were intending to offer sacrifice there, something forbidden outside the Land of Israel, and reproved them for it. The two tribes explained that it was not built for offerings, but for show: "We did this thing only out of concern that, in time to come, your children might say to our children, 'What have you to do with the Lord, the God of Israel?' . . . So we decided to provide [a witness] for ourselves by building an altar" (Joshua 22:24–26). I suspect that they were equally concerned with being able to show their own children that they belonged to the people of Israel.

Diaspora-Israel relations have never been simple. Yet this story indicates that those who seek to bring the Diaspora to an end are wasting their time. It has existed from the time Israel entered its land and will always exist—at least until the "end of days." Moses reconciled himself to the desire of these tribes not to cross the Jordan. Once he ascertained that they were not trying to cause Israel to turn away from the Land, he granted their request—but required them to keep their word to fight at the forefront of the Israelites.

Moses' requirement remains important if a true relationship is to be maintained between the communities in the Diaspora and the Land of Israel. It may not dictate actual fighting on the part of the Diaspora. But it certainly means recognizing the primacy and centrality of Israel to Jewish life, and the need to participate in the building and maintenance of Jewish life in Israel in whatever way is possible. It also means establishing ways of identifying with Israel and the Jewish people—"a conspicuous altar" if you will—preventing separation and assimilation.

Moses' charge to put "first things first" also retains its force. Whatever led Jews to the lands in which they find themselves, they must realize that there are things more important than cattle. The teachings of Judaism and the support of fellow Jews must not be ignored. And if their involvement in Jewish life should lead some of them to the conclusion that the land of milk and honey is indeed the preferred place for Jews to live, who can quarrel?

LAND OF EVIL AND LIGHT

Masei: Numbers 33:1–36:13

Susan Afterman

Those who participated in the exodus from Egypt are called the generation of the desert. And their journeys during the forty years of passage from Egypt to the Land of Israel are listed at the beginning of the last portion of the Book of Numbers, the book of "In the Desert" as it is called in Hebrew. Their life in that period was entirely defined by these journeys—the trials, hardships, and moments of revelation that occurred during each. According to the midrash in *Bemidbar Rabbah* and the medieval commentators Rashi and Ramban, the journeys were listed in the Torah to proclaim to future generations the miracles and kindness of God in sustaining a whole people that "ate no bread and drank no wine" (Exodus 34:28) all those years, far from even the most rudimentary settlement.

The late eighteenth-century commentary *Or Hahaim* says another purpose was served by the journeys. Desert places are considered by the kabbalistic tradition to be the source of impure forces, symbolized by the "venomous snakes and scorpions" to which it is home (Deuteronomy 8:15), just as Jerusalem is considered to be the source of everything in the world that is holy, the place from which blessings flow to the rest of the world. A purpose of the forty-two journeys of the people of Israel, according to this understanding, was to subdue the "great and terrible wilderness" (Deuteronomy 8:15)—that is, to subjugate the root of the evil urge. For the early journeys, before the sins of the golden calf and the spies, the saintly leadership of Moses and Aaron was enough to accomplish this. For the later journeys, the Tabernacle and its Holy Ark, in which the presence of God were revealed, were carried by the Levites. As each archetypal aspect of impurity was encountered, the children of Israel were gradually raised and made fit to enter the Promised Land.

The writing down of these journeys in the Torah, says Rabbi Shneur Zalman, the first leader of *Chabad* hasidism, in his *Likutei Torah*, gave them existence through all time. And because a positive act of the fathers brings blessings to the sons through all generations, through the merit of these archetypal journeys man has the ability to subjugate his body with its animal desires, and bring it into the service of his soul.

But it was also in the desert that the Torah was given. Many of those who received revelation were shepherds, wanderers in wilderness—Abraham, Isaac, Jacob, King David—not to mention Moses and his whole generation. Because of the lack of abundance, the extreme reduction of living things, plants and animals, the simplification of elements and details, journeying on foot through wilderness is in itself a source of understanding, of education. One is confronted with oneself and one's surroundings on the starkest level, with one's fragility in the face of overwhelming severity. There are no diversions, no business, no "background noise."

Horizons are wide. Earth and sky stand at all times in clear juxtaposition. Night is experienced as fully as day. It is easier than in settled places to experience the presence of God, to experience the physical world as forms of light. The relation of Israel with the desert did not consist only in a struggle with negative forces; it brought also an experience of unity, of the presence of God.

Jeremiah 2:6 describes the desert as something "through which no man passed, in which no man dwelled." Rabbi Shneur Zalman interprets this as implying that from a certain point of view, desert is higher than the level of man, beyond him. The essential quality that distinguishes man, Maimonides wrote in his *Eight Chapters*, is his ability to speak. Desert, where by definition man does not settle, represents the absence of speech (though the word "desert" in Hebrew is spelled the same as the word "speak"). Just as at the giving of the Torah, the people "saw the voices" (Exodus 20:15), so they saw and understood with their eyes the landscapes through which they passed: they had revealed to them the silent voice of revelation in each journey.

That desert can be experienced at the same time as the source of evil to be subdued, and as a place of revelation of the highest good, mirrors a central property of creation: "I form light and create darkness, I make peace and create evil" (Isaiah 45:7). And as, according to the midrash in both *Sifrei* and *Tanhuma*, the building of the Tabernacle was a response to the sin of the golden calf, so evil is ultimately subdued through revelation.

DEUTERONOMY

CHALLENGE TO CONVENTION
Dvarim: Deuteronomy 1:1–3:22

Blu Greenberg

Moses is about to die; Joshua will soon take up the reins. The people are at the threshold of the Promised Land. Time for a farewell speech.

Yet the Book of Deuteronomy—"the words that Moses addressed to all Israel on the other side of the Jordan" (1:1)—is more than Moses' last testament or ethical will. It is a pact between the people and God—not merely recapitulating what happened at Mt. Sinai, but renewing the covenant for a new generation.

In form, the book that begins with this week's portion resembles other ancient covenants, and its laws contain formulae parallel to legal codes of the time and region. But in classical biblical style, the way those forms are used breaks down the lines between the realms of civil and sacred and defies the West's traditional dichotomy of law and love.

Modern scholars note the likeness between Deuteronomy's form and ancient Hittite and Assyrian covenants between suzerain and vassals. These follow a standard pattern, consisting of six elements, all found here: a preamble in which the sovereign or lord introduces himself, a history of his gracious, saving deeds, stipulations of the covenant, deposition of a text, list of witnesses (often natural phenomena such as heaven and earth), and curses or blessings. The portion of *Dvarim*, for instance, provides part of the history, recounting how God led the people through the desert.

Yet form aside, the pact between God and the Jews is unique: it is not about political fidelities, but about love and law, continuously coupled; and while a sacred covenant between human and Divine, it incorporates civil law and social ethics. Deuteronomy contains two hundred laws by the traditional count, covering every aspect of life. Acceptance of the covenant, then, is no mere declaration of allegiance. It embodies a most serious commitment, that of whole-hearted observance of the law.

Scholars identify two types of ancient legal formulations in Deuteronomy and other books of the Torah: apodictic law normally begins with "Thou shalt" or "shall not," or "Whoever" or "Cursed be he who." Such statements often dealt with worship or religious action, and were normally proclaimed in public by sacred officials. Casuistic law, on the other hand, often begins with "If a person" or "When . . . , then. . . ." Such conditional law came under the jurisdiction of ordinary courts. While not falling into neat categories, the two types approximated sacred and civil law.

In Deuteronomy, though, apodictic and casuistic law exist side by side, at times in the same group of verses. Both carry the weight of God's law. The line between sacred and secular is erased: life is holistically holy.

The rabbis of the Talmud made a different distinction, based on content: laws *bein adam lehavero*, governing relations between one person and another; and *bein adam lamakom*, between human and God. Yet both, say the rabbis, really govern human relations with God. No matter that the courts adjudicate these cases; hurt your neighbor, and you violate the covenant with God.

In many a law, the connection is made explicit: "If there is a needy person among you . . . open your hand and lend him whatever he needs. Beware lest you harbor the base thought, 'The seventh year, the year of remission [of debts] is approaching' . . . and he cries out to the Lord against you" (Deuteronomy 15:7-9).

Or: "You shall not have in your bag diverse weights, large and small. You shall not have in your house diverse measures, large and small . . . For it is an abomination to God all who do such things" (Deuteronomy 25:13-16).

Observance of the law, then, becomes a measure of integrity in the covenantal relationship. And always, always, observance of law is linked to love: "And now, O Israel, what does the Lord your God require of you? Only this, to fear the Lord your God, to walk in all His ways, and to love Him and to serve Him with all your heart and all your soul" (10:12).

There are those, even today, who hold the classical Christian view of Judaism and of the law as a means to salvation. Their underlying view is that love and law are dichotomous, and that love can replace law as a way to God's grace. But a careful reading of Deuteronomy shows how inextricably linked the two are. For a Jew to say, "I will" or "I do"—and then act—is as powerful a statement of love as it is to say, "I love" or "I believe."

ENOUGH!

Va'ethanan: Deuteronomy 3:23–7:11

David Curzon

What will suffice? Moses, speaking to the children of Israel in Deuteronomy 3:23–25, says: "And I besought the Lord at that time, saying, O Lord God . . . I pray thee let me go over, and see the land that is beyond Jordan."

God refused Moses' request and warned him: "Let it suffice thee; speak no more unto Me of this matter" (Deuteronomy 3:26).

The anonymous Sages quoted in the midrash of *Dvarim Rabbah* seized the occasion of Moses' unsuccessful plea with God to consider the nature of prayer. In the middle of their discussion, the following plea of Solomon is quoted from 1 Kings 8:28: "Have Thou respect unto the prayer of Thy servant and to his supplication, O Lord my God, to hearken unto the cry and to the prayer, which Thy servant prayeth before Thee today."

The sages, noticing the distinction between "the cry" and "the prayer," comment that "prayer" in this context means praying for one's personal needs. Rabbi

Yohanan is then quoted as dismissing requests for personal needs with the observation that "no creature has any claim on his Creator." It is whatever Solomon meant by "the cry" that is fundamental to prayer.

A cry can come out of either pleasure or pain, and is the expression of a state so basic that it cannot be properly articulated. As Shakespeare observed in "King Lear" (act 4, scene 6):

> We came crying hither:
> Thou know'st the first time we smell the air
> We waul and cry.

The first whiff of independent existence produces a howl in reaction. But does this cry continue into adulthood? Tennyson, in canto 54 of "In Memoriam," thought so. He starts with an assertion of vague and uncertain faith and then proceeds to what he knows to be true and real, the cry:

> Behold we know not anything:
> I can but trust that good shall fall
> At last—far off—at last, to all,
> And every Winter turn to Spring.
>
> So runs my dream; but what am I?
> An infant crying in the night;
> An infant crying for the light,
> And with no language but a cry.

We cry out for comfort and enlightenment, but to articulate this yearning and need we have, even as adults, no language but a cry.

What are the fundamental cries? I have two candidates, the first from Psalms 22:1: "My God; my God, why have You forsaken me? Why art Thou so far from helping me?"

In other words, why do I feel alone in myself?

The second is from Isaiah 40:6–7: "The voice said, Cry. And he said, What shall I cry? All flesh is grass, and all the goodliness thereof is as the flower of the field: The grass withereth, the flower fadeth: because the spirit of the Lord bloweth upon it: surely the people is grass."

The cry here is "Death!" Why must I die?

But all this concerns only one half of existential cries, the negative ones. What are the fundamental cries of joy?

They are, of course, exactly the same. Psalm 22 moves from its opening cry of despair to a cry of affirmation: "But thou art holy."

The affirmation in response to "Why have You forsaken me?" is not that help is on its way, but that the sense of being alone in ourselves is to be regarded as holy, part of a righteous creation. This acceptance surely makes sense whether you are a believer or not. It is absurd not to accept the unchangeable, and a mark of sanity to embrace it.

And death? It, too, is to be praised. As Wallace Stevens put it in one of his poems, "Sunday Morning": "Death is the mother of beauty." Without death there would be no poignancy, no true cherishing of moments.

And now we are in a position to return to the opening of this week's portion and re-read God's response to Moses: "Let it suffice."

THE LAND'S DEMANDS

Ekev: Deuteronomy 7:12–11:25

Marc Silverman

"Beware! It's a good country." That strange warning, stated in various ways, is at the core of this portion and of the biblical view of the relation between the people and the Land of Israel. It imposes a painful, perhaps tragic burden on us, a burden which we may be carrying too long.

The Land of Israel, we're told, is "the good land" (Deuteronomy 8:7), "a land flowing with milk and honey" (Deuteronomy 11:9), a country replete with springs of water, rich in grains and fruits and natural resources. It is a land in which "thou shalt not lack anything" (Deuteronomy 8:9). But that is cause for concern, not joy. A warning usually accompanies praise of the land: Watch out, lest the land's beauty and richness, and your material achievements in it, lead you to hubris and abandonment of God's commandments. To counteract the religious and moral dangers of the land's goodness, the text underscores that its productivity is ultimately dependent on God's will and bountiful intervention:

Unlike Egypt, the Land of Israel needs rain to replenish its water resources (Deuteronomy 11:10–12).

The Land of Israel is described as a gift of the loving, covenant-making God to His people Israel. But the gift is so laden with emotions and conditions that it brings to mind the exclamation in Proverbs: "He who despises gifts will live!" God bestows it not only with reluctance, but with angry remonstrations: "Beware . . . lest when thou hast eaten and art satisfied . . . thou forget the Lord thy God . . . who led thee through the great and terrible wilderness" (Deuteronomy 8:11–15). Many strings are attached: "If ye hearken diligently unto My commandments . . . I will give the rain of your land in its season" (Deuteronomy 11:13–14). What's more, the people are told they are unworthy of receiving the gift (Deuteronomy 9:4–7).

How could have the people of Israel led more or less contented lives in the Land of Israel, while experiencing the inevitable gap between their all-too-human abilities and the Torah's covenantal demands? How could they escape being incapacitated by guilt at their inability to live up to the expectations of their relentlessly demanding and oft-outraged Father? Did they not feel doomed to inadequacy, even despair?

This sense that the land is given conditionally, that there are steep demands imposed on those who live in it, has stayed with us, though today the demands are understood in many ways. It may explain both the reluctance and even opposition of most Jews, even now, to making their homes in the Land of Israel; and the difficulties of those who live here in doing so more or less contentedly and confidently.

I have often been told by knowledgeable and committed Diaspora Jews that they prefer to dream of the perfected and redeemed "Zion" than to witness, daily, the marred and imperfect real Zion of today.

But the second problem is even greater. Many segments of the Israeli Jewish population insist that the State and Land of Israel be more than a place in which Jews attempt to build together a more or less modern, democratic, pluralistic normal society. For religious Zionists, particularly Gush Emunim, Israel has to be "the beginning of the flowering of our redemption"— a state on its way to messianic fulfillment. For other parts of the political right, it must be a Sparta, or rather a Samson, among the nations, ready for eternal warfare with implacable enemies. Some on the left demand that the state be a socialist or liberal "light unto the nations," rooted in the prophetic tradition.

According to a talmudic saying, "He who reaches for too much gets nothing." Perhaps the time has come for us to lose or at least loosen significantly our cherished "covenantal consciousness," our sense that we must be superhuman to live in the land, and begin to find our own real Jewish and human selves. Paradoxically, precisely this might let us fulfill the commandment: "And thou shall choose life."

No Guarantees

Re'eh: Deuteronomy 11:26–16:17

Yeshayahu Leibowitz

The Torah reading of *Re'eh* deals almost entirely with *mitzvot* related to public matters—with the organization of the community within a judicial and political framework in accordance with the Torah. Implicit within this legislation is a fundamental lesson about Divine prophecy and human duty.

The first *mitzvah* is the crucial one of eliminating idolatry from the Land of Israel, both the idolatry of the Canaanites and the manifestations of idolatry in the people of Israel itself—the eradication of false prophecy, of the incitement to idolatry, of the idolatrous city.

As opposed to this, we have the designation of "a place that God will choose." This is the one place in which the worship of God is to be carried out through the sacrificial cult—unlike all other places, where the worship of God is embodied by the observance of the *mitzvot* by every individual, without any sacrifices. Jerusalem, it should be noted, is not named here as "the place that God will choose." The conclusion from this, in contrast to the prevalent view in biblical criticism, may be that this instruction was given before Jerusalem had been designated the chosen site—in other words, before the time of the monarchy.

The Torah's great social legislation is expressed in *Re'eh* in the *mitzvot* regarding three institutions: the tithe for the poor; the cancellation of debts in the *shmitah* (sabbatical) year; and the general obligation to give charity. In this context two famous verses appear, and we should examine the connection—or possibly the contradiction—between them. In regard to the cancelation of debts, we are told (Deuteronomy 15:4): "There will be no poor among you, for God will greatly bless you . . ." But in regard to "not closing one's hand and hardening one's heart" (Deuteronomy 15:7) to the giving of charity, it is stated (Deuteronomy 15:11): "The poor will never vanish from the land."

The contradiction between these two verses is only illusory. "There will be no poor" is not a promise given to us, but a demand made on us. We have the duty—and the ability—to abolish poverty from our society by observing the cancelation of debts and all the other *mitzvot* with social significance. Without these provisions, which we are obligated to enforce, the other verse will remain true. In no social system will poverty disappear by itself. One should not trust to it disappearing through the One who "opens His hand and satisfies the needs of every living creature" (Psalms 145:16). It is God's will to make us responsible for abolishing poverty among us.

It is a grave error to understand the Torah and the Prophets as implying that God's promises will be fulfilled regardless of our behavior. A Divine promise is not like the prediction of a pagan oracle, an astrologer, or anyone else who claims miraculous knowledge of the future. A Divine promise is always a demand made of man: This is the way things ought to be. And thus *Tosafot* (a major commentary on the Talmud from the thirteenth century) understands prophetic promises, with profound significance for faith: "The prophet predicts only that which should be" (*Yevamot* 5a)—with no certainty that this is what *will* be. This rule applies even to the vision of the messianic redemption: It is what should be, but whether it *will* be depends, at least to some extent, on us.

This applies to the verses concerning poverty: it is fitting that there should be no poor, but there is no guarantee of this, even though the Torah says that "God will bless you." The blessing is conditional on us doing everything we are obliged and able to do in order to get rid of poverty; otherwise, the apparent promise will not be realized. And the same pertains to the destiny of the entire Jewish people. Amos, Jeremiah, Ezekiel all promised that the ten tribes would return from exile and rejoin the Jewish people—and the promises were not fulfilled. That does not undermine our faith in "the prophets of truth and right." They prophesied what should be, but we were evidently not fit to have these promises fulfilled.

DIRECT RESPONSIBILITY

Shoftim: Deuteronomy 16:18–21:9

Blu Greenberg

A corpse is found in an open field, the victim of violence. No family claims the body. The killer can not be
found. What must be done?

Says Deuteronomy 21: Distances to the surround-
ing cities must be measured. Elders and judges of the
nearest city are obliged to bring a calf that has never
borne a yoke to an uncultivated wadi and there kill
it by breaking its neck. The young calf, the pristine
setting, and the manner of death are stark symbols of
life brutally cut off. The elders then wash their hands
and swear their innocence: "Our hands did not shed
this blood, nor did our eyes see."

Implicating these respected leaders seems outra-
geous. The Talmud (Tractate *Sotah*) asks: "Would it
cross our minds that the elders are murderers?" Yet the
charge is not murder but idly standing by. The elders
must swear, says the Talmud, that "he did not come
to us and get sent away without food and hospitality;
we did not see him [go somewhere dangerous] and let
him go unescorted."

The first lesson of this law is that leaders are en-
trusted with setting the moral tone of a society. Thus,
they can be held responsible for a social climate in
which a person can go unnoticed, in which no one cries
out "Halt!" to the murderer or "Look out!" to the victim.

Respected elders might not sully their hands with
murder. But in any culture, they may be guilty of caring more for property or power than people. They are
guilty unless they can swear that they tried their best
to create a humane society, one that protects the weak,
the outsider.

We Jews know this well from the Holocaust. When
Pastor Trocme of Le Chambon set the tone, by sermon
and example, for his small French community, five
thousand Huguenots managed to save five thousand
Jews, despite a continuous Nazi presence in their town.
When the Polish church excluded Jews from its concern, all but a few extraordinary Christians turned on
them.

This notion applies to every structure with a hierarchy. In some institutions, everyone seems caring; in
others, the entire bureaucracy seems designed to frus-
trate. The difference lies not in the human material,
but in the ethical stance that is taken at the top and
seeps down.

Israel's army is a case in point. Despite the excesses
of a few, its moral fiber is unmatched. How do so
many nineteen-year-olds act with maturity and restraint while facing barrages of stones and curses? Why
are its victories unmarred by rape? Because such stan-
dards matter greatly to the leadership and are commu-
nicated to the rank and file.

On the other hand, why is it that in the traditional
community so many Jewish women suffer the status
of *agunot*, wives whose husbands refuse to divorce
them, when a reinterpretation of Jewish law could set
them free? Here, too, the tone is set at the top, by rab-

binic authorities and religious court judges who don't care enough about women's lives to right the wrongs.

The law of the calf has a second lesson: A leader may not be a bystander. And there is no dispensation for "disaster fatigue," or allowance for valuing one human life less than another. Says the Torah: This victim, a stranger without family or friends—even from him you may not distance yourself. You cannot say "I'm not responsible" or "I've seen too much of this," or "I don't even know him."

"Don't get involved"—that is the usual way out, for individuals and governments. But it is unacceptable. Surely history will convict the leaders of Europe and the United States who continue making bland statements over the cries of the victims in Bosnia. Where are the government leaders? Have too many scenes of violence jaded the world?

Leaders, like ordinary people, must order their priorities. Surely, they cannot do everything, all at once. But the Torah tells a leader always to bear in mind: You are responsible for the character of the society you lead; and the moment you have the power to help "the other," you are directly responsible.

YESTERDAY, MADE NEW

Ki Tetze: Deuteronomy 21:10–25:19

Dov Berkovits

The English philosopher Bertrand Russell was fascinated with the power of the immutable past. In his autobiography he muses about our inability to alter our personal pasts or history: "The Past is an awful God, though he gives Life almost the whole of its haunting beauty." In my student days, I found that Russell's enlightened agnosticism was tainted by this near-deification of the past. In its profound determinism, Russell's belief that the past cannot be changed is a relic of paganism.

The Talmud, in Tractate *Yoma*, provides an alternative to Russell's awe of the past—one that is crucial for understanding *teshuvah*, the choice to turn one's life toward God. It cites two teachings quoted in the name of a single sage, then tries to reconcile them. "Resh Lakish said, 'Great is *teshuvah*, because it transforms intentional sins into unintentional sins.' But didn't Resh Lakish say, 'Great is *teshuvah* because it transforms intentional sins into meritorious deeds'?" Both, the Talmud explains, are correct: *teshuvah* motivated by fear makes the sin unintentional; motivated by love (of God or Torah), it makes the sin into a positive act.

Resh Lakish understood that past, present, and future are not objective domains, independent of each other. Time is a dynamic process, permeated and shaped by God's word. Human consciousness and speech are active agents in this process, fashioning the past, building the future, creating new life and naming it, as God did.

Modern Jewish writers have also dealt with the Jewish sense that time and consciousness are interwoven. In his *Zakhor: Jewish History and Jewish Memory*, historian Yosef Hayim Yerushalmi describes this approach as not being concerned with the "historicity of the past" as much as with "eternal contemporaneity." Our past and future, personal and communal, are alive, ever existing in the present. In a similar vein, Gershom Scholem wrote of the twin attitudes of the Jewish commentator to the Torah—unspeakable awe of the text along with apparent presumptuousness to interpret the meaning and application of revelation in the present.

The past, then, is refashioned in our present lives. That recognition, however, should not be restricted to moments of *teshuvah* or Yom Kippur prayers. It should alter daily life, allowing us to build a Jewish present out of the "eternal contemporaneity" of Torah. The alternative is abdication of the Jewish present and, with it, alienation from the past and the future.

The abdication of the Jewish present can clearly be seen in our all-too-common attitude to many of the commandments in the Torah portion of *Ki Tetze*. The medieval work *Sefer Hahinukh* counts seventy-four commandments in this portion, more than in any other portion. They touch on almost every aspect of life. If Torah is for living and not just learning, these *mitzvot* should belong not only to a dead past, but should shape and be interpreted by the Jewish present.

The questions *Ki Tetze* creates are many: What form would a Jewish penal code and prison system take? Can a high-tech, investment-oriented economy function without taking interest? What approaches to environmental issues would reflect the commandment to send away a mother bird before taking her child or the ban on cross-breeding species? How should holiness in sexuality and marriage be expressed in a society in which men and women share productive roles? Or more pointed: How many of us stop our cars to help others stuck by the side of the road, or take time to seek out owners of lost objects we've found?

To some, a creative culture that reflects a Jewish concept of time might appear to be a pipe dream. But the issues raised in the everlasting present of *Ki Tetze* are critically relevant. Today, even among those who are capable of studying the detail and the depth of these *mitzvot*, many are oblivious, indifferent, or unbelieving as to their practical import.

In contemporary Jewish life, very few believe anymore that sanctifying the fullness of the present is a realistic goal—not the Orthodox, the Conservative, or the Reform, the ultra-Orthodox or the secular, Gush Emunim or Peace Now. There are myriad forms of Jewish mysticism, scholarship, prayer, ideologies, denominations, but very little Jewish present, shaped by the mutable past. Is Torah learning capable any longer of creating society? Can we explore our past to change and refashion life? These are the key issues of contemporary *teshuvah*, of turning toward God.

FEARING THE WEAK

Ki Tavo: Deuteronomy 26:1–29:8

Tzvi Marx

Moses foresees that when the people of Israel enter and settle in their land, they will face new dangers of failing to keep the covenant. "When you come into the Land" (Deuteronomy 26:1), he believes, the newly won comforts and illusion of security will lead to new patterns of moral and religious deviation, beyond those known in the desert.

So in his final exhortations to the desert-bred generation, he instructs them to conduct a "beachhead" ritual as soon as they cross the Jordan. Fundamental offenses against the covenant will be singled out and the people publicly warned against them. This mass outdoor event centers on a litany of select curses and blessings to be declaimed by the Levites standing in a valley and alternatively facing Mount Ebal and Mount Gerizim. The tribes, six on each mountain, are to respond to each pronouncement with a resounding "Amen" (Deuteronomy 27:15–26).

The curses, as we would expect, are directed against overall, primary violations of ethics and faith—idolatry, dishonoring parents, sexual perversions, trespass against property, and violent crimes. Cursed is he who "removes his neighbor's landmark" and he who "subverts the rights of the stranger, the fatherless, and the widow." Yet between these two is a warning against a transgression that seems somewhat out of place in such a list: "Cursed be he who misdirects a blind person on his way" (Deuteronomy 27:18). Why should a sin that affects only a small minority, and which hardly seems a temptation to anyone but the most malicious, rate such a high profile in the covenant?

The blind, however, are among the most obvious of the disabled people in society. And the disabled, like aliens or people without family, are paradigms of vulnerability. Weakness is regarded as a stigma, inviting exploitation and even revulsion. Robert Murphy, a quadraplegic anthropologist, notes in his book *The Body Silent* that "the physically impaired often arouse, in varying degrees, revulsion, fear, and outright hostility—sentiments that appear to be spontaneous and 'natural' because they seem to violate our values and upbringing." Hence the special need for the instruction "not to insult the deaf, nor place a stumbling block before the blind" (Leviticus 19:14).

In contrast to the human attitude, the Psalmist says that "God opens the eyes of the blind." A midrashic comment gives this an eschatological meaning, pointing to the handicapped as specially deserving for their moral achievements, given the obstacles they must overcome.

Yet it may be disconcerting to recall that even King David, the hero of redemptive hope, harbored an instinctive revulsion for certain types of handicapped people. When he conquered Jerusalem, he gave an order that "those who attack the Jebusites shall reach the water channel and [strike down] the lame and the blind, who are hateful to David" (2 Samuel 5:8).

Rabbi Jacob Ettlinger of nineteenth-century Germany, in his responsa *Binyan Tzion*, explains that the 2 Samuel text, understood literally, allows us to admire David for subsequently overcoming this weakness. David commands that Mephibosheth, the only surviving son of his beloved friend Jonathan, be given the hospitality of the king's house and even of his own table, though he was lame in both feet (2 Samuel 4:4, 9:13). David's action can be seen as a moral achievement in which intimacy, familiarity, and commitment allow a person to overcome revulsion. Learning from this example today should lead us to consider adopting the approach of "mainstreaming," integrating the disabled into the wider community, rather than separating them. Through the familiarity of day-to-day contact, people can overcome their fears of the handicapped.

Upon entering the land, the people have the opportunity to create a moral society according to the covenant. Such a society must enable all its members to be really present in the land by including them all in its life, and by refusing to exploit or humiliate the weak and disabled as a cheap way of gaining advantage or experiencing achievement. The prohibition on misleading the blind, therefore, is not a footnote. It is a cardinal point of the covenant.

IT DEPENDS ON EACH OF US

Nitzavim: Deuteronomy 29:9–30:20

Barry W. Holtz and Bethamie Horowitz

In the Jewish calendar the Sabbath before Passover carries a special name, *Shabbat Hagadol*, the "great" Sabbath; and the Sabbath between Rosh Hashanah and Yom Kippur is called *Shabbat Shuvah*, the "Sabbath of Repentance." Oddly, the Sabbath before the New Year does not carry any special designation. Despite its anonymity, the last Sabbath of the year is a weighty one, and here the Torah portion of *Nitzavim* always falls. The time of year creates a special lens through which the portion's words are refracted.

For us, *teshuvah* has come to mean personal change. So it is somewhat surprising to see that the Torah portion placed before Rosh Hashanah speaks about the community as a collective: "*Atem nitzavim hayom kulkhem*"—"You [plural] are standing this day, all of you ..." (Deuteronomy 29:9).

Yet *Nitzavim* fits the time of year in a number of ways. First, although this passage is about the Israelites listening to Moses, we, too, are standing before

God. The experience of the Days of Awe is a challenge for a community as a whole—all of us, our families and friends and others whom we may not know, the "regulars" in *shul* and those who come only at the High Holidays.

Second, there is verse Deuteronomy 29:13-14: "It is not with you alone that I make this covenant . . . It is with the person who stands with us this day . . . and also with the person that is not here with us this day." Those "not here with us this day" are future generations. We are dealing with what we nowadays call "Jewish Continuity"—the future of the Jewish people. And the portion suggests that the things we do at this time of year—the *teshuvah* we are challenged to make—do not just affect us as individuals, but the whole of the Jewish people, of today and of the future. That, in turn, says something about the meaning of community.

Continuity, the future of the Jewish people, is not only a matter of counting the numbers: "You shall listen to the voice of the Lord your God to keep His commandments and His statutes which are written in this book of Torah" (Deuteronomy 30:10). Being Jewish has a content that Jews have always called Torah. How that Torah is to be understood has changed in different times and places. But being Jewish has always entailed a connection to that content.

Furthermore, living a life that takes Torah seriously is not an unrealizable ideal, beyond the reach of the community or of the individual, today or in the past: "For this commandment which I command you this day is not too hard for you, neither is it far off . . . but the word is very close to you, in your mouth and in your heart" (Deuteronomy 30:11-14). When we think about our own *teshuvah* and about the future of the Jewish community as a whole, the idea of acquiring Torah, of living a life that is deeply connected to Torah, is not some impossible task. The text itself, and the rabbis later on, present Torah as an obligation of the entire community—one that is attainable by everyone, not just the few.

It's interesting to note that while *Nitzavim* begins with "you" in the plural, when we reach the most quoted verse in the portion, "Therefore choose life" (Deuteronomy 30:19), the verb is in the second person singular. The act of *teshuvah* appears to rest with individuals, as in the latter verse. But the context tells us that individual repentance is only part of the story. The choices the Torah puts before us also show this: "life and good, death and evil" (Deuteronomy 30:15). Rashi points out that "life" depends on "good" and that the following verse links both to "loving the Lord and keeping God's commandments . . . then shall you live and multiply." The individual choices we make affect the future of the community and how the generations "multiply" over time.

As we enter the days of awe and self-reflection, may each of our individual efforts at *teshuvah* bring life and goodness for the entire community—in the present and in generations that follow.

HOLLOW VISION, LOST STATECRAFT

Vayelekh: Deuteronomy 31:1–30

Micha Odenheimer

What is religion? A set of personal beliefs meant to help
people generate, privately, the faith required for living
in the face of suffering, disappointment, and death? Or
a vision meant to transform social and political reality, as well as individual hearts and minds?

In the modern West—especially in countries, like
the United States, that have been influenced by Prot-
estantism—religion has largely been relegated to the
private realm. But the Torah clearly intends to create
a holy society, not just holy individuals. Many commandments—choosing a king, setting up cities of refuge, observing the Jubilee year—are to be fulfilled by
an entire nation. And the *mitzvah* of *hakhel*—"gather" or
"congregate" in Hebrew command form—is intended,
at least partly, to drive this home. The *mitzvah*, given
in Deuteronomy 31:10–13, calls for the entire people
of Israel, "men, women and children," to congregate
every seven years, at the end of the sabbatical year,
during Sukkot, to hear the king read the Torah at the

215

Temple. The gathering, a reenactment of the giving of the Torah at Mt. Sinai, is a reminder that revelation addresses a society congregated in a unified whole.

If we had a king and a Temple today, we, too, would be required to fulfill the commandment of *hakhel* after each sabbatical year. In fact, just over a century ago, Rabbi Eliyahu David Teomim, an early religious Zionist leader, published a booklet calling for creating a ceremony that would serve, in the absence of king and Temple, as a reminder of *hakhel*.

Only after Israel's establishment did his suggestion reach a wider audience. His grandson, Rabbi Binyamin Rabinovitz Teomim, published a book containing the original pamphlet, along with essays by great religious Zionist rabbis of the time. The timing was no coincidence. A central tenet of religious Zionism had been that renewing Jewish political independence would free the Torah from the bonds of exile, allowing it to address social and political questions over which Jews had no control when ruled by gentiles. *Hakhel* symbolized the Torah's return to the public sphere.

The vision of religious Zionist thinkers was not only ceremonial. The best of them began to rethink the social, political, and economic basis of modern life using the Torah as their guide. Perhaps the finest example came from Rabbi Shimon Federbush, who in 1949 published a terse volume called "Israel's Statecraft." Erudite and convincing, Federbush presents a vision of economic and social justice rooted in the Torah.

But even the most advanced students at today's religious Zionist institutions have probably never heard Federbush's name or studied the issues he broached, because religious Zionism all but abandoned its broad agenda. By agreeing to the creation of a separate Ministry of Religious Affairs whose mandate was limited to marriage, divorce, and ritual, religious Zionists virtually admitted that such areas as labor, justice, and immigrant absorption were outside their mandate.

David Ben-Gurion's own secular version of prophetic Judaism was so authoritative that it overshadowed all others in the state's early years. But since the 1970s, and even more so in the last decade, this vision has been hollowed out; the public sphere has been dominated by the drive for economic growth at all costs. Meanwhile, the gap between rich and poor in Israel keeps growing. The arms industry, though necessary for Israel's security, continues to sell to corrupt regimes. And Israel's ecological balance and the beauty of its open spaces are threatened by a near-hysterical race to build roads and industries throughout the country.

There has been one major exception to religious Zionism's ceding of public concerns to the secular state: Gush Emunim's efforts to determine the country's borders. Agree or disagree with Gush Emunim's goals, one must recognize that Gush Emunim is almost all that remains of the ambition to push Torah beyond ritual into the public, political sphere.

Yeshayahu Leibowitz, the sharp-tongued Jewish philosopher, once predicted that when Israel withdrew from the West Bank and Gaza Strip, disappointed Gush Emunim followers would convert to another religion. I see hope for another scenario: that when peace comes, the idealism that ignited Gush Emunim will be turned to the task of making Israel the kind of state that earlier religious Zionists dreamed it could be.

DESOLATION

Ha'azinu: Deuteronomy 32:1–52

Pinchas Giller

Like characters in a musical, Biblical figures are apt to step outside the narrative and break into song. So Hannah does, in exultation upon the birth of Samuel (1 Samuel 2:1–10), or Jonah when he expresses faith from the fish's belly (Jonah 2:3–10).

In the biblical "musical," the song is called a prayer and is presented in the familiar style of a psalm. But these extemporaneous prayers have only a vague connection, in their content, to the events of the narrative. Perhaps Hannah and Jonah spontaneously began to recite popular prayers of their day.

In the Book of Psalms, on the other hand, what otherwise might appear to be general prayers are linked to crises in the life of the psalmist, such as "A Victory Song of David, when he fled before Saul in the cave" (Psalm 57), "A Psalm of David, when he was fleeing before Absalom his son" (Psalm 3), or "A Hymn of David, when Nathan the prophet came to him, after he had been with Bathsheba" (Psalm 51). Expressive poetic prayer, biblical spirituality teaches us here, is often situational. It is based on a character's existential condition, what he or she is going through at the time.

When Moses steps forward to begin his parting song in the Torah portion of *Ha'azinu*, he knows that he is going to die, and has come to remonstrate with the people of Israel, in a last surge of Deuteronomic moral rage. Primordial figures—the elders and officers of the people, the very heavens and earth—are his witnesses (Deuteronomy 31:29), "for I know that after my death, you will become degenerate, straying from the path which I have commanded you." The whole Book of Deuteronomy is his farewell oration; the final song is a testament to the inevitability of human inadequacy. Moses is literally singing for his life, denying, through images of eternality, his impending death.

The song portrays God as a rock, nurturing yet unyielding (Deuteronomy 32:4, 18, 30, 31). God is the Father-Creator (32:6) who finds the people of Israel as desert orphans (32:10) and nurtures them with an eagle's feral obsession (32:11). As the triumphant master of nature (32:13), God draws enormous fecundity from the arid, unforgiving land, "suckling with honey from the rock, oil from flint," raising fat, complacent, bovine children (32:14).

Israel's response is to turn to the degeneracy of paganism and the occult (32:17). The song expresses classical prophetic astonishment at the emptiness of pagan belief, calling its object a "non-god." God's response is to afflict Israel with a "non-people" (32:21) and then, when Israel is wholly decimated, to exclaim "I, I am He, there is no god besides Me, I kill and I bring to life, I wound and I heal." This truth is expressed in an orgy of blood and vengeance, the triumph of God's "flashing sword" (32:41), and "arrows drunk with blood" (32:42).

A hairdresser in Berkeley once told me that the biblical God often seemed like an alcoholic parent. It was painful to hear, because I knew she had been reading closely. Certainly God's response to the song itself is brutal: "Go up onto Mount Nebo . . . and die on that mountain . . . for you dishonored me, and did not sanctify me . . . from afar you will see the land where you will not go" (32:49–50). Moses' silent acceptance of this judgment is the mute perversity of the codependent.

As prophecy, the song in *Ha'azinu* is as personal as the anguished cries of Jeremiah, an expression of Moses' dispossession. The song is altogether relevant to Moses' condition. As God will bring rough justice to Israel, so Moses must pay for his transgression. He will die orphaned and alone, hounded by the memory of his own inadequacy and unacceptability, doomed to the alienation of exile, with the terrible knowledge that it is his own fault.

THE CHOICE

Vezot Habrakhah: Deuteronomy 33:1–34:12

Susan Afterman

Abraham's entry into the Land of Israel is linked un-
equivocally with blessing: "Go out from your country
. . . from the house of your father, to the land I will
show you. And I will make you a great nation, and bless
you and make your name great, and you shall be a
blessing" (Genesis 12:2). But the passage of the Children of Israel into the Land of Israel is associated only
conditionally with blessing. Throughout Deuteronomy,
Moses reiterates the choices before his people. If, when
settled in the land, they keep God's commandments,
if they walk in His ways and fear Him, they will be
blessed. If, once they eat well and live in good houses
and their wealth increases, they forget Him; if they say
in their hearts, "My own power brought me to this
place"; if they serve other gods, they will be cursed. But
why did Moses feel the need to repeat the warnings
over and over?

On the face of it, the choice that was required of that
generation, and one can't help adding, of ours, seems

an easy one: "Look, I put before you today life and good, death and evil" (Deuteronomy 30:15). But, according to the nineteenth-century kabbalistic commentator Rabbi Shlomo ben Haim Hikel, known as the Leshem, to choose "life and good" is not so easy. For "the inclination in the heart of man is evil from his youth" (Genesis 8:21), and even the righteous cannot withstand the evil urge completely (Ecclesiastes 7:20). For this reason, the rabbis of the Mishnah concluded that "it would have been better for man had he not been created" (*Eruvin* 13:2).

The righteous patriarchs, says the great medieval commentator Rashi on Genesis 32:5, subliminally accepted the Torah even before it was given, and observed its commandments, and thus merited blessing. But, Rashi says, while the Israelites of the generation of the desert received the Torah in its revealed form and said, "We will do and hear," they did not do so of their own free will. Mount Sinai itself had been held over their heads in threat to secure their agreement, he says, understanding Exodus 19:17 as saying "they stood under the mountain." It was only at the end of the first exile to Babylon, on Purim, that the Jews achieved voluntary acceptance of the Torah, as can be understood from Esther 9:27, "The Jews carried out and took upon themselves and upon their seed . . ." So when the people were on the verge of leaving the desert to enter the land, their willingness to live according to the Torah was very much in question. Nobody knew this better than Moses, who had witnessed frequent backslidings, including the sins of the golden calf and of the spies.

And it was in this context that Moses stood on the last day of his life and blessed the tribes: knowing only too well their weaknesses; facing the knowledge that he himself, because of them, would not enter the Promised Land that he had prayed so many times to enter.

This blessing is recorded in the last portion of the Torah, which is read together with the first verses of Genesis on Simhat Torah, completing the yearly cycle of Torah readings. "And this is the blessing that Moses, man of God, blessed the Children of Israel before he died" (Deuteronomy 31:3). According to Ramban and other medieval commentators, the word "this" is itself the blessing, as is written *"This* is from God, and it is wonderful in our eyes" (Psalm 118). For "this" is understood by the midrash in *Dvarim Rabbah* to refer to the Torah itself, as is written: *"This* is the Torah that Moses put before the children of Israel" (Deuteronomy 4:44). That is, Moses blessed them with the Torah—that they would in the end cling to the Torah, and thus to life itself. And according to the Ramban, because of the great merit and stature of Moses, the man of God, whatever blessing he gave will come to pass.

Moses, therefore, was not only the channel through which the Torah descended into the world. Because of the potency of his blessing, not only the righteous but all of us will in the end merit to choose "life and good," and will in turn, through our own actions, bring into being the blessings associated with living in this land. As Rashi reads Deuteronomy 33:28: "And Israel will dwell, each one in safety, like Jacob, in the land of corn and wine, whose heavens drip down dew."

SPECIAL READINGS

COINS AND THE REALM

Shkalim: Exodus 30:11–16

Menahem Froman

Has the establishment of a Jewish state solved the problem of freedom of the Jewish individual? Or has it merely raised the problem again on a different plane? It is a question to ponder on *Shabbat Shkalim*, the first of four special Sabbaths leading up to Pesah, the festival of freedom. The additional reading, Exodus 30:11–16, describes how each adult male of the people of Israel is commanded to give half a shekel for the building of the sanctuary.

Thus, the commentators explain, a census was carried out. With each person contributing a set amount—"the rich shall not give more, and the poor shall not give less"—the sum would reflect the number of contributors. According to Rashi and others, God commanded us not to number the people in any other way. They cite the census that King David took, described in 2 Samuel 24 as a grave offense deserving severe punishment. David himself recognizes this, repents, and says to God: "I have sinned greatly in what

I have done." The parallel text, 1 Chronicles 21:1, relates even more explicitly: "And Satan stood up against Israel and moved David to number Israel."

This conviction persisted in later generations. A direct cause of one of the first Jewish revolts against Roman rule was the fierce opposition to the census carried out by the emperor who had resolved to turn Judea into a Roman province.

To be counted by the emperor meant belonging to his kingdom. In other words: accepting his dominion. And to accept the dominion of a flesh-and-blood monarch was perceived by the Jews as throwing off the yoke of the King of Kings. The late Professor Ephraim Urbach, the renowned authority on rabbinic literature, once commented that the Jewish conception of a mortal king as being among those "other gods" whose worship is forbidden in the Ten Commandments was borne out in the Roman period, when the reigning Caesar was worshiped as a deity.

But even when the ruler was not regarded as divine, Jews saw subservience to a ruler as negating the service of God. And the objection was not merely to foreign subjugation, as a comment in the Jerusalem Talmud (Tractate *Brakhot*) shows: discussing the verse "Hear, O Israel, the Lord our God, the Lord is One" (Deuteronomy 6:4), the rabbis point out that a slave is incapable of performing the commandment of accepting the yoke of Heaven—because he has another master. There can be only one Lord. Israel, the rabbis say, was freed from Egypt to be servant of God and therefore may not be slaves to anyone else.

This is why King David was forbidden to enumerate his people—they were not his possession. The Jewish conception is summed up in Gideon's words to the men of Israel: "I shall not rule over you, neither shall my son rule over you; the Lord shall rule over you" (Judges 8:23). Samuel warns the children of Israel in great detail of the dangers of appointing a king, and concludes: "And you shall cry out in that day because of your king . . ." (1 Samuel 8:18).

Later, when David bows to practical exigencies and establishes a royal dynasty, he is confronted with an almost insoluble problem: how to establish his rule in such a way that it will not conflict with his people's religious obligation not to subjugate themselves to a human being.

It is a problem that continues to confront us to this very day. Having liberated ourselves from foreign dominion, we must recognize the dangers that even the civil framework poses to our freedoms as we build our own sovereign state.

THE DISPOSSESSED

Zakhor: Deuteronomy 25:17–19

Gershom Gorenberg

Around the time of the Lebanon War, I had a rented room in the elegant old Jerusalem neighborhood of Rehaviah, and often found an empty seat at an ornate, comfortable synagogue where the regulars included cabinet ministers, top officials, and their soon-to-be-Knesset member sons. Each Friday night a different congregant gave a short talk on the week's portion. On the Sabbath before Purim, I dreaded the sermon. The Book of Esther says Haman was the descendant of Agag, king of the Amalekites; the special reading for that Sabbath recalls how Agag's ancestors ambushed the Israelites in the desert, and commands us to "erase the memory of Amalek." Given the *shul* and the mood of the day, I feared a tirade identifying Amalek with a present-day enemy, and drawing ugly conclusions.

A thin, balding figure rose for the sermon. I couldn't remember ever seeing him in the synagogue before. But as I expected, he roared: "The Torah demands of us, 'Erase the memory of Amalek from under the heaven; thou shalt not forget!'" I sighed.

"But this is a strange commandment," he went on. "How can we both 'erase his memory' and 'not forget'? And why should the commandment apply specifically 'in the land that the Lord thy God gives thee for an inheritance'?

"To understand, we have to look at how Amalek came into the world. Who was the original Amalek, founder of the nation?

"In Genesis 36, we learn Amalek was the son of Eliphaz, the son of Esau—the man who was dispossessed of his birthright and robbed of his paternal blessing by our father Jacob.

"The midrash, in *Breshit Rabbah*, reveals the price paid for Esau's hurt and resentment. When Esau learned he had lost the blessing, says the Torah, 'He cried with a great and exceedingly bitter cry.' The midrash cites the one other verse in the Bible where those words repeat: Mordechai responds with just such a cry to the decree against Jacob's children—by Haman the Amalekite."

I leaned forward. This wasn't what I'd expected.

"But Amalek inherited resentment from his mother as well," he said. "The Gemara says in Tractate *Sanhedrin*: 'Timna was a daughter of kings . . . She sought to convert. She came to Abraham, Isaac, and Jacob, and they would not accept her. So she went and became the concubine of Eliphaz the son of Esau, saying: It is better to be a handmaid to this nation then a noblewoman elsewhere. From her came forth Amalek, who caused sorrow to Israel. Why? Because they need not have turned her away.'

"And be precise here: Timna was Eliphaz's concubine. We know the fate of a concubine's son—to be a second-class child, not accepted by the sons of his father's wives, an outsider, with no place in the will, no inheritance."

The man at the podium bellowed: "Such was Amalek: the third generation of those we and others turned away, dispossessed, made outsiders—the heir only to resentment and anger. That's what created the bitter tribe that attacked us in the desert when we were faint and weary.

"Therefore, to erase Amalek's memory, we must make certain not to recreate our worst enemy. For those to whom we deny their birthright, those whom we discriminate against, leave out—they become the new Amalek.

"When does our obligation fall on us most fully? When we are in our land, when we have received our own inheritance. And even here, we cannot simply 'erase the memory of Amalek' once and for all; we must guard ourselves eternally: 'Thou shalt not forget.'"

He slipped back into the pews. I wondered how the self-possessed, powerful men around me had understood his message.

After the service, I couldn't find the speaker in the crowd. In the months to come, I would look for him in the *shul*, but I never saw him again.

BEYOND COMPREHENSION?

Parah: Numbers 19:1–22

Baruch J. Schwartz

We admire an interpretation of the weekly Torah reading when it is philosophically or morally relevant. Yet
we often feel instinctively that such interpretations are
far from the original meaning of the biblical text. We
may feel enriched by the thought, but we know how
to read, and we know that the text neither says nor
implies it.

But when we're presented with a historical interpretation, one that elucidates what the text meant in its
own time, place, and culture, we're apt to feel disappointed. We may find it more faithful to the text, but
it's neither edifying nor applicable. And those of us
who regard rabbinic tradition as part of an unbroken
chain of revelation are liable to view as a threat the
suggestion that the Bible's original intent might differ
radically from the sages' interpretation.

And so, the more existentially "true" an interpretation, the more distant it seems from biblical Israel; the
more faithful it is to the original intent, the further it

seems from us. It appears that the Torah can either be
understood on its own terms, or it can be eternal, but
not both. This dilemma is more pronounced when the
text deals with ritual laws, particularly sacrifices. How
can it be that the best way to make sense of the law as
stated in the Torah is to see it as firmly rooted in the
beliefs and practices of the ancient world? Have a hundred generations of homiletical and rationalist exegetes
been "wrong"?

The law of the red heifer—the *parah* of the special
reading of that name—is the classic case: taken in its
original context, it says that a corpse produces defilement, contagious to all who come in contact with it or
even come under the same roof. And one who fails to
rid himself of this defilement, by means of the reddish
mixture of water and the ash of the heifer—symbolizing sacrificial blood but sprinkled on the person, not
the altar—will contaminate the sanctuary, the abode of
God's presence.

The law is eminently intelligible if taken as a pecu-
liarly Israelite rite of sanctuary purgation, and it embodies the sublime idea that Israel's God will dwell
among and protect His people only if they keep defilement—death and all its manifestations—away from His
abode.

And yet what the text clearly says was not considered
reasonable in the time of the sages. The dynamic power
of defilement, and the intrinsic efficacy of ritual, were
no longer admitted. Thus, even the great first-century
sage, Rabban Yohanan ben Zakkai, was at a loss to explain the rite to his students: "By your lives, the corpse
does not defile, nor does the mixture of ash and water
cleanse. The purifying power of the red heifer is simply a decree of the Holy One." His comments, which
have become the authoritative word on this week's special reading, are based on the premise that the rite can-

not be comprehended, that it is a *gezerah*—an inscrutable Divine edict, simply to be obeyed.

His words are edifying: A law which is not readily understood must be kept anyway. But the comment also expresses frustration with, and rejection of, the thought system of the ancient world in which the law was actually given. Only the first interpretation articulates the belief contained in the text. The idea suggested by the second, that God's laws are often unintelligible, is foreign to biblical thought. Only the second reflects an idea which became normative in post-biblical Judaism; the Judaism of the sages rejected the idea that physical defilement is an actual threat to communal existence. Perhaps the eternity of the Torah is upheld when both are admitted to be "correct."

HYSSOP'S FABLES

Hahodesh: Exodus 12:1-20

Reuven P. Bulka

It's hard to stay humble—especially when a person or a group, in the grip of fervor and joy, takes a step forward in life. The special reading of *Hahodesh* speaks of such changes, as does the Torah portion of *Tazria*, with which it is read in some years. They are further united by an implied reminder of the need for humility.

The *Hahodesh* reading gives instructions for the Pesah offering. *Tazria* deals with *tzara'at*, rendered in English as "leprosy" but actually a variety of ailments. Common to the mechanics of the sacrifice and of purifying the "leper" is the herb hyssop. Maimonides, in his *Guide for the Perplexed*, admits he does not know why hyssop was used in either rite. Here, perhaps, is a solution to Maimonides' dilemma:

When God gave Moses the instructions for the paschal sacrifice, he didn't mention using hyssop; He merely said the Israelites should take the blood of the sheep and put it on the doorposts and lintel. Moses, apparently on his own, added that the blood should be applied with a bunch of hyssop. Putting the blood on the doorposts was an act of defiance. By using the blood of an animal considered a god in Egypt, the Israelites proclaimed the cult to be mere idolatry. Showing defiance was important not for its own sake, but to establish in the people's minds that they were free of Egyptian bondage and idolatry, physically and emotionally.

But there was a danger that self-assurance might lead to arrogance. Possibly for this reason, Moses told the elders to dip the bunch of hyssop in the blood and then apply it to the doorposts. The hyssop, traditionally considered the lowliest of plants, was meant to inspire humility. Moses thus tried to balance the act's defiance with the humble procedure through which the act would be accomplished.

Hyssop also figured, together with cedar-wood and a scarlet dye made from a worm, in the procedure through which the person with *tzara'at* was readmitted to society. The great medieval commentator Rashi suggests that the cedar is symbolic of arrogance, and that it is counterbalanced in the reentry rite with the dye of the worm and the hyssop, both of them lowly species. The message thus expressed was that the process of reentering society must be characterized by humility.

The individual, now publicly relieved of his affliction and the object of considerable attention, might well be tempted to flaunt his restored status. The Torah, in introducing the hyssop into the reentry, is perhaps gently saying: We welcome you back into the group without qualification—but take care that you conduct yourself with due modesty.

This is a potent message to those in our generation who have made the very significant reentry into Judaism, those *hozrim bitshuvah* who in seeing or being shown the light have reembraced their Jewish heritage and begun observing Jewish law. In returning, it is always best to come back with hyssop in hand, to act with humility—even in the excitement and exuberance of having "discovered" Judaism.

HOLIDAYS

EXTRAVAGANT FORBEARANCE
Rosh Hashanah

Moshe David Tendler

"Shame is essential to the repentance process," wrote Rabbenu Yonah of Gerandi in his thirteenth-century moral treatise, *Gates of Repentance*. He explained: "Would one not be ashamed to sin in the presence of others? Should you not be ashamed that you have sinned in the presence of God?"

Today, though, we have lost our sense of shame for our own sins, and with it, our indignation at those of others. We have become nonjudgmental. Three factors can be blamed for this unresponsiveness. One is the breakdown of families, and the urbanization of society that has all but destroyed the sense of community. We live in a world of strangers. As a result, we have learned to see no evil, but have not committed ourselves to do no evil.

Second, the horrors of the Holocaust have made all other sins pale in comparison. Inhumanity is no longer newsworthy; cruelty is regarded as natural in this pre-messianic era.

Third, the consequence of democratic freedom has been the introduction of a new inalienable right—the right of privacy. As an expression of the democratic spirit, we have developed an apathetic forbearance for evil. We really do not care enough to be ashamed—or angry.

"Mind your own business; everyone can do his own thing"—that has become the new ethic of our society. What embarrasses or shocks us today? Adultery, incest, white-collar crime, violation of fiduciary trust, child abuse? When reported in the newspapers, these hardly receive more than a glance as people turn to the sports sections or the supermarket ads.

The AIDS epidemic provides a clear example of the failure to feel anger or shame. Innocent recipients of tainted blood transfusions are living question marks. But how did the charitable blood transfusion become a lethal weapon? A major mode of AIDS transmission is an activity referred to in the Torah as "an abomination, punishable by death." It is theologically abhorrent; it menaces our lives and those of our children. Yet we refer to homosexuality with the euphemism, "an alternate lifestyle." Many states in America have legislated anti-discrimination laws to compel forbearance and prohibit the expression of indignation at those who engage in this "lifestyle."

This is not the way of Torah. "Rebuke your fellow man" is a commandment that must be followed if we are to develop a moral society. Failure to express rejection means condoning such behavior. The proper attitude of responsibility toward other human beings is reflected in Jewish law's instruction to a physician treating a dying AIDS patient who contracted the disease through homosexual activity. Speaking of the case of a dying person "who has completely left the path of Torah law," the *Shulkhan Arukh* instructs the doctor not to condone his behavior. But the continuation of the ruling can be summarized as follows: "I, God, command you to console this poor sinner, risk your life to preserve the little life that he has left. Comfort him, try to heal him, but express your shame and indignation at his behavior."

During the Days of Repentance beginning on Rosh Hashanah, as a prerequisite for gaining God's forgiveness, we must seek forgiveness from others for our transgressions against them—and be willing to forgive them. Granting such forgiveness implies forbearance for others' actions. However, forbearance is a double-edged sword. It cuts away the barriers that prevent individuals from loving and respecting each other, but it also can sever the nerves that sensitize us to evil. Moral indignation has its place in a loving relationship. Rebuke is an expression of lovingkindness, as is forbearance of idiosyncrasies.

The Torah commands us to speak no evil of others. We must give the benefit of doubt to all, lest we accuse the innocent. Yet we are also asked to be observant of the behavior of those about us, and to assume the difficult burden of rebuking our fellow man. That equilibrium is but one part of the Torah's instructions for building families and society that foster respect for all who are created in God's image.

The Terror of Compassion
Yom Kippur: The Book of Jonah

Gershom Gorenberg

Noah was a tight-lipped man. Told the world would end, he neither argued with God nor set out to warn and reprove people. Told to build an ark, he got his saw and hammer. Lost on a shoreless sea, he voiced no prayer. Perhaps he wasn't the type to ask questions. Perhaps, having seen Adam's children fill the pre-flood world with thuggery, cattle-thieving, and knife brawls, he saw no reason to urge God to be merciful or to give humanity the chance to repent. Even when the dove he released faded into the rainbowed sky and life began again, Noah kept his mouth shut.

Such silence makes the imagination itch for commentaries and retelling, for midrash. One of the first rewrites comes in the Bible itself, in the Book of Jonah. The writer imagined an anachronistic Noah, in his own urban Middle East, and a man hardly as accepting.

Jonah's name, meaning "dove," points to the link. The center of his story, like that of Noah's, is a journey across the waters, which would swallow him but for Divine rescue. The apparent theme of the tale is Divine judgment: "Yet forty days, and Nineveh will be destroyed," Jonah says (Jonah 3:4), echoing, "And the rain was on the earth forty days and forty nights" (Genesis 7:12). And the reason for wrath is the same. Noah's generation was sentenced for robbery, *hamas* in Hebrew, the marriage of violence and theft, as is written: "The end of all flesh is come before Me; for the earth is filled with robbery" (Genesis 6:13). This is also Nineveh's sin, for its people are saved when they "turn every one of them from his evil way, and from the robbery that is in their hand" (Jonah 3:8).

Robbery, as the medieval commentator Ramban explained, is a rational matter; moral philosophy, *sans* revelation, will tell people that it is sin. Both Noah and Jonah face people bereft of the Torah's revelation, which is to say the gentiles, or more simply, the world, generic humanity. Noah sees humanity's doom, then becomes the father of the seventy nations of the world. Jonah is sent to proclaim the end not to the Israelites, but to the world, scaled down to the one teeming metropolis of Nineveh, capital of his century. He has been transplanted from the age of myth, when a whole world could end, to an ironic present complete with seaports and the need to pay his own fare.

Jonah, too, is a reduced figure, uncertain and fitful in place of obedient, facing a God whose demands and intent are much less obvious than those of Noah's Deity. Jonah is sent to reprove—"Arise, go to Nineveh, that great city, and cry against it, for their wickedness is come up before me" (Jonah 1:2)—but the Divine sentence is left for him to deduce. Rather than accept the quixotic mission, he quite reasonably turns and runs. He travels the sea to escape God, not to submit to Him; rather than being master of a ship of refuge, he is the sole passenger thrown into the waves so that the others may be saved. Then, literally from the depths, he turns and prays aloud.

Then comes the key reversal: Noah watched universal death and accepted God's ways; Jonah watches as Nineveh swiftly repents and God forgives, and he declares, "It is better for me to die than to live" (Jonah 4:3). The story doesn't work out as Noah's did, for Jonah comes after Noah, after God promised never again to bring destruction. Once God ruled by strict justice, an eye for an eye, havoc for havoc. Now he shows "pity on Nineveh, that great city, in which are more than sixscore thousand people who cannot discern between their right hand and their left, and also many beasts" (Jonah 4:11).

As the midrashist who wrote the Book of Jonah understood, it's Divine compassion, not justice, that makes us "greatly angry" (Jonah 4:4). Strict justice provides a simple calculus of reward and punishment, which Noah can silently accept. Forgiveness lets the wicked, the exploitative, the technicians of brutality go unpunished— frequently even without Nineveh's repentance—so that the innocent suffer. Mercy makes God incomprehensible, erratic, and leaves us moderns, like Jonah, so often "greatly angry, even unto death."

REJOICE IN YOUR VULNERABILITY

Sukkot: Leviticus 22:26–23:44

Paula Hyman

Autumn is the season of ambiguities. The weather is still warm, and nature has yielded her bounty of grain and fruit. Yet, the rawness of winter—the season of scarcity—suggests itself in the chill of the morning air. The festival of Sukkot that occurs (as the *Shabbat* reading during the holiday tells us) at the time of *tekufat hashanah*, the turning of the year, gives us an opportunity to acknowledge, and celebrate, the uncertainties of autumn, and of life.

Sukkot began as an agricultural holiday of thanksgiving that marked the final harvest of the year. The four species that we bring together in the *lulav* and *etrog* reinforce the agricultural theme, as does the booth itself, which derived from the huts built in the fields for tired harvesters. But the holiday reading from the Book of Leviticus already adds a historical motif: God declares that we are to dwell in booths "in order that future generations may know that I made the Israelite people live in booths when I brought them out of the land of Egypt" (Leviticus 23:43).

The humble *sukkah* hardly seems an appropriate symbol of God's protection. In fact, in Tractate *Sukkot* of the Talmud the rabbis debated whether the *sukkot* in the wilderness were actual booths or clouds of glory with which God surrounded the wandering Israelites as a shield. Yet the temporary and simple nature of the actual *sukkah* is a powerful signifier of the vulnerability of human beings, whether desert nomads some three thousand years ago or city dwellers today. The *sukkah* reminds us that all homes are ultimately impermanent and that our fate is contingent on factors beyond our control. The Book of Ecclesiastes that we read on the *Shabbat* of Sukkot reinforces this message of the transiency of our existence with its cry that "all is futile."

The *sukkah* has provided yet another lesson to rabbinic interpreters throughout the generations. At the time of harvest thanksgiving, the season when we have the most, we are told to live in a *sukkah* and make do with little. The *sukkah* signals the need for modesty, pushing us to remember a period in our history of material deprivation. As the twelfth-century commentator Rashbam put it, "And lest you should say in your heart, 'My own power and the might of my own hand have won this wealth for me' (Deuteronomy 8:17), it is the practice to go out of houses full of good things at the time of the ingathering, and to dwell in booths, in recollection of those who had no inheritance in the wilderness and no house to dwell in."

In our own age, Rabbi Mordecai Kaplan suggested the psychological benefit that remembering the simpler way of life in the wilderness through the ritual of living in the *sukkah* provided to the Israelites settled in Canaan, and presumably to us as well. By detaching ourselves, however temporarily, from the material world that we take for granted, we are able to develop a critical stance toward it.

Yet, with all its cautionary lessons about pride and vulnerability, materialism and vanity, Sukkot is *zman simhatenu*, the time of our rejoicing. In the holiday calendar of Leviticus that we read on Sukkot, it is the only festival about which we are specifically commanded to "rejoice before the Lord your God . . ." (Leviticus 23:40). As the epitome of festival joy, it was familiarly known by the rabbis as *hehag*—that is, *the* holiday.

There is a tension between the joy of the Sukkot festival and the vulnerability symbolized by the *sukkah*, a tension that the holiday implicitly affirms as a necessary component of the human condition. Only when we have accepted the limitations of our existence can we express fully our joyous gratitude for our lives and their blessings.

MEASURELESS MERCY

Sukkot—Intermediary Sabbath: Ecclesiastes

Gershom Gorenberg

Our world—the real one, without deluges, cities ham-
mered by fire and brimstone, and other acts of mythic
justice—is immensely indifferent to us: "One generation goes and another generation comes, and the earth
is forever unchanged. The sun also rises and the sun
sets, and rushes to the place where it'll rise again . . .
All the rivers flow to the sea, and the sea is not full,"
says *Kohelet* (Ecclesiastes 1:4–8), and adds: "Everything
is tiresome, a man cannot even speak it."

The very modernness of that ennui is enough to
prove *Kohelet*'s claim that there's nothing new under
the sun. One can easily imagine this biblical author
in a room in Pamplona at night, drunk, bitterly tired,
saying with Hemingway: "I did not care what it was
all about. All I wanted to know was how to live in it."
For, as *Kohelet* says, if the world doesn't care a whit
for us, if nothing is ever new, "What profit has a man
of all his toil under the sun?" (Ecclesiastes 1:2).

With such ideas, reports the midrash in *Kohelet Rabbah*, Ecclesiastes almost didn't make it into the canon. Once the book was sanctified, the sages had to labor mightily to make it fit the faith. "What benefit do the righteous have in piling up *mitzvot* and good deeds?" asks the same midrash, rewording *Kohelet*'s question. One answer it predictably gives: The righteous will be rewarded in the world to come, when God "will make their faces shine like the sun." Another answer puts the reward here and now: "Rabbi Levi said . . . 'It's enough for them that I make the sun shine on them.'"

But Rabbi Levi's answer isn't quite satisfying, as another midrash shows. Alexander the Great, recounts *Breshit Rabbah*, once traveled "beyond the mountains of darkness" to learn how a king named Katzia passed judgment:

> He sat with him one day. A man came and complained about his fellow, "This man sold me a ruin and I found a treasure in it . . . I bought a ruin, not a treasure."
>
> And the seller said, "I sold the ruin and everything in it."
>
> The king said to one of them, "Do you have a son?" and to the other, "Have you a daughter?"
>
> "Yes," they said.
>
> "Marry them, and they'll have the wealth."
>
> Alexander looked on, amazed . . .
>
> Katzia asked, "How would you have ruled?"
>
> "I'd have killed him and him, and the kingdom would have taken their wealth."
>
> Asked Katzia: "Does the rain fall in your place?"
>
> "Yes," said Alexander.
>
> "And the sun shines?"
>
> "Yes."
>
> "Do you have sheep in your place?" asked Katzia.
>
> "Yes."
>
> "Damn it all, not for your sake does the sun shine or the rain fall, but for the sake of the sheep," said Katzia . . .

The midrash then quotes Psalms 36:7, "Man and beast you save, O Lord," explaining, "Man you save for the sake of the beasts." A nice answer, but the implication is perilously close to *Kohelet*'s complaint: The sun shines, and what we do below does not matter.

For another perspective on that existential griev-ance, look at the story of Noah. It begins with a more responsive and just world: ". . . and the earth was full of violence . . . for all flesh had corrupted its way on earth. And God said to Noah . . . I will destroy them with the earth" (Genesis 6:11–13). Humanity's acts beneath the sun were evil, and God responds by bring-ing "the flood of water upon the earth to destroy all life . . . from under heaven." The sun ceases to shine, and the sea is far more than filled.

Once the catastrophe ends, though, God makes a one-sided covenant with humanity: Regardless of how people behave, "I will not curse the ground again for man's sake . . . While the earth remains, seedtime and harvest, and cold and heat, and summer and winter, and day and night will not cease" (Genesis 8:21–22).

The words could nearly be *Kohelet*'s: The sun will rise and set, seasons will continue, the heavens will not spill punishment or reward. Yet after the deluge—after even imagining the deluge, imagining a universe of strict justice—everything looks different. What was once tire-some beyond words now speaks of mercy. For the world stands on mercy—immense, unjust mercy.

OCEAN OF LIGHT

Hanukkah

Micha Odenheimer

In the spiritual geography of the Jewish year, whose contours are shaped by the weekly Torah portion, Hanukkah inhabits a landscape filled with dreams. On the Sabbath preceding the holiday and the Sabbath of Hanukkah itself, the Torah portions tell of Joseph's dreams, Pharaoh's dreams, Joseph's rise to power through dream interpretation, and finally of the twists of plot leading to fulfillment of Joseph's youthful dreams.

The *Sefer Yetzirah*, an early kabbalistic text, says the month of *Kislev*, when Hanukkah is celebrated, is the most propitious time of year to affect changes in how one sleeps and dreams. And in the section of Talmud, in Tractate *Brakhot*, that tells us how to bless God for personal miracles—how to celebrate one's own private Hanukkahs—the text suddenly shifts to a lengthy discussion of dreams and dream interpretation.

What do miracles and dreams have in common? Both are often interpreted as signs, symbols, heralds, both are experienced as moments saturated with meaning. Both are also eruptions from a realm usually hidden. Since at least the time of Freud, dreams have been considered revelations from the subconscious. Miracles are also a bursting forth of light into our "normal" world, the world ruled by rigidly enforced laws of nature.

But if we sense the subconscious as a realm of darkness, we intuit the place from which miracles emerge as an ocean of light hidden from view. "Well-known are the words of Nachmanides in his commentary to Exodus," writes the late Rabbi Yitzhak Hutner, the most original and profound of ultra-Orthodox philosophers of recent years. "From open miracles we learn about miracles that are hidden in the actions of nature itself. Nachmanides says . . . that one who does not believe that all of nature is made up of hidden miracles has no portion in the Torah of Moses!" Hutner explains Nachmanides' remarks by reminding us of the primordial light that the midrash (in *Breshit Rabbah*) says filled the universe when God said "Let there be light." This light, by its very nature infinite in its scope, allowed Adam to see "from one end of the world to the other." When it was shining, the laws of nature, which are essentially limitations, had no power.

This primordial light has been hidden away "for the enjoyment of the righteous in the future to come." Yet it is not absent today. It retains its lifegiving potency; hidden, its workings continue. A miracle, says Hutner, is simply a perforation in the screen concealing the primordial light. At the place of the perforation, where the pinprick of light pours in, the laws of nature—which are the obscuring material of that screen—simply cease to exist. And if all the seemingly limiting laws of nature are a cover beyond which an infinite light is concealed, the same is potentially true of the darkness of the subconscious itself, including its most anarchic dreams.

The Talmud's discourse makes it clear that the meaning of a dream depends as much on the characters of the dreamer and the interpreter as it does on the dream's manifest content. But when the dreamer is worthy, and the interpreter of the highest spiritual level, even dreams that seem to be rooted in the dark areas of the subconscious can augur illumination. After a discussion of dreams that clearly indicate a dreamer whose subconscious has internalized devotion ("One who recites in his dream 'May His great Name be blessed forever and ever'"), the Talmud offers some startling interpretations. "Whoever has intercourse with his mother in a dream," it says, "should expect [to be suffused with] Divine understanding, as is said, 'For you will be called a mother to wisdom.' [a radical reading of Proverbs 2:3]. Whoever has intercourse with his sister in a dream should expect Divine wisdom, as is said, 'Say unto wisdom you are my sister' (Proverbs 7:4)."

The twenty-fifth word of the Torah—Hanukkah falls on the 25th of *Kislev*—is "light" in the Divine fiat, "Let there be light." Rabbi Pinhas of Koretz, a friend of the Baal Shem Tov, says that in proclaiming the miracle of Hanukkah, the Hanukkah candles cast forth light from the infinite, hidden storehouse of primordial illumination. This light has the power to make our dreams transparent, so that we can see through them the radiance of God.

DEFEAT IN DISGUISE

Purim: The Book of Esther

Seymour Epstein

A king, an evil vizier replaced by a good one, a harem girl picked to be queen: it's a classic tale of Persian court intrigue, usually understood as portraying a clear Jewish victory. But close reading of the Book of Esther reveals a defeat of the Jewish spirit by a majority culture. The enemy turns out to be not Haman, but the slow-working force of Persian culture.

In a book that never explicitly mentions God, King Ahasuerus is referred to over two hundred times. Ahasuerus's palace is decorated with trappings reserved elsewhere in the Bible for the desert Tabernacle and the Temple in Jerusalem: God's houses.

Implicitly, the text contrasts this fool of a king, drunk for his key decisions, with the King of kings. While the Biblical God can be persuaded by mortals to change his actions, the king of flesh and blood cannot rescind his own edicts. So we read (Esther 8:11): "The king permitted the Jews in every city to gather together, to defend, to destroy, and to murder . . . all the forces . . .

that assault them, children and women." A previous
royal decree permitted the Jews' destruction; now the
only way to prevent the massacre is to give them per-
mission to kill those who threaten them. In the empire
of exile, men have greater powers than God—and the
constant potential to abuse them—while God, omni-
present in biblical Israel, is conspicuously absent.

In chapter 2, Mordechai and Esther are introduced.
The writer stresses that Mordechai comes from a solid
Jewish family in Jerusalem, and the Hebrew root for
"exile" appears no fewer than four times in one verse.
And the names! In exile, the hero uses a Mesopotamian
name connected with the chief Babylonian god, Mar-
duk. The heroine's Hebrew name is Hadassah; but she
is known as Esther, from Ishtar, that beautiful Babylonian goddess. Parallel, in our day, would be reading
of a hasid who goes by "Christopher."

Exile's influence on Jewish values is complex, erod-
ing them unevenly. Mordechai does nothing to prevent his cousin, Esther, from entering the queen con-
test, telling her only to hide her Jewish identity. But
when Haman climbs the court ladder to a position that
demands a bow from others, Mordechai refuses. When
would it be better to demonstrate Jewish values—in
preventing one's cousin from sleeping with a Persian
king, or in balking at showing diplomatic courtesy?
Esther's actions involve several transgressions of Jewish law; bowing would break no letter of the law, foreign as the gesture might be to our spirit.

After Haman's decree of destruction, Mordechai de-
cides it's time for Esther to act as a Jew. But Esther, it
becomes apparent, knows nothing of the threat to her
people—and her only concern is to avoid embarrass-
ment at court. Her answer to Mordechai's plea for help
is refusal to approach the king, based on court protocol. When Mordechai earlier discovered a plot against
the king's life, the information passed from him to

Esther and on to Ahasuerus in the space of one verse. But with the lives of her people in danger, Esther turns shy. She acts only after Mordechai tells her (Esther 4:13–14): "Do not think that you alone in the king's house will escape the fate of all the Jews. For if you are silent this time, relief and rescue will come to the Jews from another place, and you and your father's line will perish." This is effective consciousness-raising—but comes from the same man who had told her to hide her Jewishness.

The pair's victory again reveals a lack of biblical values among the Jews of this upside-down world. The Jews celebrate with yet another round of boozing, all too characteristic of their Diaspora culture. Where, for example, are the prayers to God?

The conclusion must be that this story was written to illustrate the effects of exile and, by implication, point to the merits of Jewish autonomy in our own land, under the influence of transcendent values and laws.

Why, then, is Purim celebrated as a victory? It's possible that a satire written in the Land of Israel was later misread by Jews in exile with a more "sophisticated" view of the Diaspora. More probable is that the masquerade, the burlesque, the parodies of Jewish texts that are part of Purim celebration are themselves signs that this particular victory is tainted with irony. We are told to get so drunk that we cannot distinguish between Mordechai and Haman. That, precisely, is the ambiguous message of Purim.

FROM THE NARROW PLACE
Pesah: The *Haggadah*

Gershom Gorenberg

We are, of course, the most free people in history. We can live where we want (even if the cars, streets, and shop signs make a thousand neighborhoods look the same); we can do what we want (though some days the choice seems to be between which brand of peanut butter to buy); we can believe what we want (even if few people believe anything with a passion that grips their lives, and those few, we know, are eccentrics).

"In every generation, a person is obligated to see himself as if he went out from Egypt," says the *Haggadah*, "as is written, 'for the sake of this, the Lord acted for me when I went out from Egypt.'" It's easy to read on quickly, thinking of the historical Egypt and even of a metaphorical one, a country or a time in which our parents or grandparents did not have our freedoms.

Read more slowly:

In every generation, a person is obligated to see himself . . . To find yourself in the retold story, to relive it, you have first to see yourself. In the grand meta-

phors—Egypt as the Pale of Settlement, Egypt as the
days of Jew-badge and ghetto—we see history, but can
forget ourselves. "Where are you?" God asked Adam
(Genesis 3:9), knowing well the answer, knowing well
that Adam did not; the *Haggadah* repeats the question.

As if he went out from Egypt . . . Understood as a word,
not a name, the Hebrew for Egypt means "the twice-
narrow place." It is a place of constraints and claustro-
phobia, a passage so constricted that a man or woman
can only walk forward, from the given past to an un-
avoidable future, without being able to turn. "From
the narrow place I cried out, Lord," says Psalm 118,
using another form of the word, "in the wide place the
Lord answered me." Egypt is a condition of the spirit;
see yourself, and you may see your Egypt. And then
comes the act of imagination that the *Haggadah* demands: to see yourself leaving, coming out from the
river-cut walls of the canyon into the open plain.

The difficulty in imagining this may be what our
age shares with the real Egypt. Dying, Joseph told the
Israelites: "God will surely remember you" (Genesis
50:24). Not only did a king arise who knew not Joseph,
but a generation of Israelites arose who knew not his
promise of redemption. Or perhaps they knew it, but
took it no more seriously than the rantings of an anar-
chist great-aunt—as out of place as any message of
a better world in our *fin de siècle* cynicism—because
Egypt was the pinnacle of civilization, and its society
was the given order, if not the perfected order.

As if he went out . . . Imagine going, acting, and not just
being taken. The Exodus began when, after decades of
silent acceptance, "the children of Israel groaned from
the servitude and cried out" (Exodus 2:23). The cry
could come only when those in the narrow place imagined that there could be something, somewhere else;
only then did Moses arrive, bearing a vision that could

now be heard. "He who wakens to purify himself," says the Zohar in another context, "is helped."

But the cry was not enough. Still in Egypt, the Israelites had to slaughter lambs and spread the blood on their doorposts. Sheep were worshiped as gods in that country, says the midrash in *Shmot Rabbah*. Only he who had decided to go free could commit the heresy of that sacrifice and smear the evidence where all could see. To go out, he had to take the first step inside Egypt.

   . . . As is written (Exodus 13:8), "for the sake of this the Lord acted for me when I went out from Egypt." In the biblical context, "this" refers to *matzah*. Countless mistranslations have made the verse say that we eat *matzah* "because of what the Lord did" in the Exodus. Ibn Ezra's commentary gets it right: God took us out for the sake of eating *matzah*—that is, for the sake of fulfilling his commandments. Those who leave the "twice-narrow place" are not only freed *from* adding bricks to Pharaoh's massive, meaningless cities, but freed *to* accept a system of meaning for life.

On this night, we leave Egypt. What place are you leaving; where will you go?

Spring Elopement

Pesah—Intermediary Sabbath: The Song of Songs

Daniel Landes

The Song of Songs delivers what a true love story always promises. It graces the lover—and reader—with both the carnal and the spiritual. Interpreters have either reduced the Song to a series of romantic ditties—and haven't quite explained what it is doing in the Bible; or they've accepted it as the metaphor for the relation of Israel to God, shamefacedly fleeing the bodily realm. But romantic love in the Song is neither the only reality nor merely a useful metaphor. It rather is the paradigm of a true relationship. One must enter the earthly to reach the Divine.

The tension that propels the Song is that despite their great desire for each other, the Shulamite maiden and her mysterious beloved continually elude one another. They seek each other out for brief trysts, then separate only to start again. What is their problem?

The Shulamite describes herself as beautiful within. Her sunburned visage betrays a life lived and suffered for others (1:6): "My own vineyard I have not kept."

Seeking her beloved, she is told he is out with the graz-
ing sheep. There the lovers find each other for a short
outdoor, springtime assignation (1:16–17):

> Our couch is a bower; cedars are the beams of our house,
> Cypresses the rafters.

Neither this meeting nor one in the "house of wine"
(2:4) lasts. But the beloved wishes to make the relationship permanent, and urges her as he peers through the
lattice of her house (2:13): "Arise my darling / My fair
one, come away!"

The Shulamite spurns the offer of elopement—but
not her lover. She rises in the middle of the night and
searches the deserted streets. Braving danger and abuse
from the city guards, the Shulamite finds her beloved
(3:4):

> I held him fast, I would not let him go
> Till I brought him to my mother's house,
> And into the chamber of her who conceived me.

And yet, he leaves at the crack of dawn. The Shulamite
believes she can compel the beloved to live in her reality. This he resolutely refuses to do. He wants no part
of her mother's house or bed.

So we are left with two stubborn personalities, deeply
in love but poles apart. She complains that he is not
present—always leaping from hill to hill. He is chagrined
that she is holding back (4:12):

> A garden locked
> . . . A fountain shut up
> a spring sealed.

Even as she waits for him one damp night, they miss
each other's cues; when she finally responds to his

entreaties to let him in—"I opened the door for my beloved / but my beloved had turned and gone" (5:6).

At the end, we have the impression that the two will eventually unite. The Shulamite breaks the impasse, confessing (7:11), "I am my beloved's" *ve'alai teshukato*—literally, "and his desire is upon me." This can only be understood as her own acceptance of the beloved's deep-seated desire. "Come, my beloved," she says (7:12), "let us go into the open/let us lodge among the villages!" The Shulamite now understands the relationship will only flower if she will abandon everything and join her beloved in a mutual journey of discovery, both of the land and of the life that they might build there together. She must leave the comfort of her mother's home and even the oppressive security of her brother's vineyards.

And is this not what the Israelite soul says on Passover, in final ecstatic surrender to God, its Beloved (7:11,13):

> Let us go into the open . . .
> there I will give my love to you!

A MOMENT OF MIRACULOUS SURVIVAL

Pesah—Seventh Day: Exodus 13:7–15:26

S. Ben-Tov

Once there was a plan to line the Suez Canal with enormous plastic bags containing cordite. If the Egyptians invaded—this was proposed before the Yom Kippur War—the cordite would be ignited. Combustion would puff up the giant bags, and a tidal wave of displaced water would roll over the invaders.

The Suez Canal proposal was a brainchild of ex-members of the Palmah Science Corps—a group of scientists and engineers chiefly at the Weizmann Institute, who in 1947 began to develop weaponry. Their Biblically conceived idea shows how Israel's builders looked habitually toward our ancient history and myth. Like all cultural cliches, this one hides its own truth.

When human beings set out to create something completely new—be it technology, art, or a family—we look for the new creation's meaning in our origins, as the word "original" suggests. Fresh inventions "carry in them the pulse of the distant source," writes critic George Steiner. The Suez Canal plan, a technological solution, was also a cultural solution to the problem of being who, and where, we are. It was remembering the exodus from Egypt—a declaration of faith.

What kind of faith does the Song of the Sea (Exodus 15) evoke?

Timing, and a sense of timing, is the key to the miracle that the Song depicts. In most of the Song, the sense of time is one of exultant history: the recent miracle, "Pharaoh's chariots and his host has He thrown into the sea" (15:4), is the logical precedent to the future crossing into Canaan: "All the inhabitants of Canaan shall melt away . . ." (15:15). But in lines 8–11, which describe the Red Sea crossing, time narrows to immediacy. The waters part. Yet we, the listeners, are not permitted to see the Israelites cross between the suspended water-walls. Instead, we hear Pharaoh's ferocious threats: "The enemy said, I will pursue, I will overtake . . . I will draw my sword, my hand shall destroy them" (15:9–10). Then the waves fall and silence him.

Why has all our attention been directed to the enraged Egyptians as our ancestors flee? Why, in the moment of rescue, are we forced to relive their nightmare of being pursued?

Jewish history is full of cataclysm, a word whose Greek root means "washing-away." Often, the violent waters of cataclysm have closed over our heads. By the drama of its timing, the Song reminds us that between the divinely suspended waters, our survival hung in the balance. The Song's heart is a moment of survival: miraculous, never to be taken for granted.

I learned about the Suez Canal proposal after my father died, when his friends from the Science Corps gathered and reminisced about the times they had shared. My father had fled to Palestine in 1941, as a teenager. In 1947, he showed up at Weizmann, during a heat wave, wearing a winter coat under which he toted an improved rifle. European immigrants learned to keep silent about the Holocaust: my father had survived both his parents, and never talked about it. After his death in a plane crash that killed two hundred people, I had a dream. I was shouting "Lord of the Universe, where were You when my father died?" On waking, I was disheartened by the thought that millions of people—including my father while he lived— might have dreamed a similar dream.

My dream's question is answered, perhaps, by the Song of the Sea. Through its poetic power, we are taught a retrospective faith. God is present in our words, the songs and stories that connect us as an enduring people across history's intermittent devastations. When we repeat the stories of Jews who survived to record them, God is present; when we record our stories, we invoke God's presence for our children. God is present for me in my father's friends' tales and in my stories about him. While such faith is not a perfect consolation, it is enough.

Recorded words always presume a future; and the songs passed down by those who survived to sing have the power of making us believe in the future. Significantly, the Song of the Sea reenacts the crossing twice: first we relive the miracle of our survival. Then, after the Israelites' song about the triumphant future, the crossing reappears, showing what we did not see before: "For the horse of Pharaoh went with his chariots and his horsemen into the sea . . . but the children of Israel went on dry land in the waters of the sea" (Exodus 15:19). So the Song ends. As we repeat it, our nation becomes visible to us, walking on dry land.

BREAD AND DESTINY
Counting of the Omer

Zeev Dashevsky

Plain barley is feed for beasts. Bread is food for human beings. The former was offered in the Temple at Pesah; the latter at Shavuot. The progression between the two—from a basic, almost animal existence to the life of a human being—symbolizes the spiritual development of the Jewish people, from the assembly of slaves who departed Egypt in haste to the people gathered at the foot of Mount Sinai to receive God's word. That progression is reflected in the counting of the *omer* between Pesah and Shavuot, between the festival of freedom and the festival of the giving of the Torah.

A leading contemporary Orthodox thinker, Rabbi Joseph B. Soloveitchik of Boston, described the experience of the Exodus as forging the Israelites into one unit through a "covenant of fate." The people had suffered together, they shared a common fear, and together they witnessed God's miracles. They were objects of the same forces beyond their control. As a group bonded by fate alone, however, they were not yet ready to enter a dialogue with God. That spiritual link was achieved on Shavuot, with the receiving of the Torah, which inaugurated what Rabbi Soloveitchik called a "covenant of destiny." Now, of their own free will, they join a partnership with God that will shape their future.

The development of the people from a community of fate to a community of destiny is chronicled in the Torah and its commentaries. God nurtures a spiritually primitive society, making it a nation ready to receive the Torah. In Exodus 17, when the people complain at Rephidim that they are thirsty, God tells Moses, accompanied by the elders, to journey to Horeb to "smite the rock" for water. According to the midrash, they already knew that Horeb was where the Torah would be given. The point is clear: both basic physical needs (water) and spiritual development come from a common source— and that source is outside the realm of their immediate experience. Through their bodily concerns, the people are being introduced to the spiritual.

It is this development from the community of the Exodus to the community of Sinai that is hinted at by the word *lirtzonkhem* (your will, your volition) in Leviticus 23:11, the verse describing the bringing of the *omer*. The grain offering was to be waved by the priest as an expression of the will of the people. The will, it is hinted here, marks a high point in the development of character. Jewish history, ancient and modern, can be seen as a movement toward the creation of a full human will, above the impulses of nature. The Israelites coming out of Egypt, like all living creatures, had *ta'avah*, physical urges. But *ratzon*, intelligent volition, marks their elevation to humanity in the fullest sense. The special significance of the *omer* ceremony is that the people have acquired a will; only now can they be worthy of a dialogue with God that will determine their destiny.

The historical-spiritual development that we mark so carefully during this period has its parallel in modern times and its commemorative days. Holocaust Day, Israeli Independence Day, and finally Jerusalem Day all fall within the Counting of the Omer. The period of bondage in Egypt is paralleled in our century by the cry of a suffering people facing physical destruction, which we recall on Holocaust Day. Just as the Exodus marked the time when the children of Israel became free, the establishment of the state, commemorated on Independence Day, marked the creation of a sovereign political entity to ensure physical survival. And Jerusalem Day, the anniversary of the city's reunification, should also symbolize a spiritual step toward "the rebuilt Jerusalem" of our prayers.

The question asked by the Israelites soon after leaving Egypt, "Can God be in our midst?" is still heard in the midst of our people. As we approach Jerusalem Day, may we strengthen and purify our national will and prove worthy of that all-important partnership of God and Israel symbolized by Shavuot.

ARE WE STILL ISRAEL?

Shavuot: Exodus 19:10–20:23

Dov Berkovits

A particularly hopeful development in Israel–Jordan relations after the peace accord was an Israeli proposal for educational exchange and consultation. But Jordan's education minister rejected the idea, declaring that Israeli culture was too superficial to offer anything to centuries-old Arab culture. Putting aside the possibility that the Jordanian minister spoke as a xenophobe, Pan-Arabist, or fundamentalist, it's worth considering, on the eve of Shavuot, the image of Israel reflected in his comment.

Has, in fact, the culture of the People of the Book become an aggressive Levantine version of plasticized American consumerism? Has Zionism been reduced to the aspiration to turn Israel into the Singapore of the Middle East? Abba Eban wrote—when Sinai was still a formative if secularized Jewish reality—that the Jews gave humanity the notion of "civilization." For three thousand years, the creative tension between the People and the Book generated philosophy and law, offered models of piety and morality and defined a discipline leading to personal commitment and humility and to communal compassion. But as we move towards the Jubilee of Jewish statehood, how do we as the People of the Book view ourselves? Do we know ourselves as Israel? Do we have a vision of how to use our Torah as a tool to build society?

Saadyah Gaon claimed that Israel was a people by virtue of the Torah. Who reads Saadyah today to learn from him, to argue with him? Maimonides believed that Abraham's life could serve as a model for all humanity. How many Israeli high school graduates know of the glory of Maimonides, of his impact on medieval philosophy and on the meaning of "Israel" to this day?

* * *

When the Jews returned to Jerusalem after the seventy—year Babylonian exile, as described in the Book of Nehemiah, they faced formidable economic and security challenges, similar in many ways to those faced in the formation of modern Israel. When the ancient returnees to Zion achieved a modicum of security and independence, they held a national convocation to renew the covenant between God and Israel. The assembly of nearly fifty thousand made a common commitment to refrain from intermarriage, to deepen love for fellow Jews, and to participate in filling the needs of the newly built Temple. It also gave the Second Commonwealth of Israel its underlying identity for the next six hundred years, as the revelation of Sinai had earlier given the destiny of Israel among nations its original conception.

In contrast, in the modern Third Commonwealth, a modicum of security and independence has only deepened the confusion regarding Israel's destiny. The Jewish state has struck its covenant not with Sinai but with Western, democratic tenets. As critical as these principles may be for safeguarding the political process in

a modern state, they are at the root of deep ambiva-
lence in the Jewish psyche. Do the tenets of human
equality necessarily imply denying the uniqueness
of Israel among the nations? Do liberalism's limits
on authority and society's turn toward humanism
imply that the term "Israel" is to be emptied of Divine
sanctity? What practical meaning does the Sinaitic covenant have in a Jewish democracy, beyond providing
democracy and humanism with a religious terminology and a *kashrut* certificate?

* * *

The Ten Commandments begin with the words "I am
[*anokhi*] the Lord your God who took you out of Egypt."
Of the two Hebrew pronouns for the first person singular, *ani* and *anokhi*, the latter intimates the stronger
sense of being and presence—"I *am*." The Divine utterance of *anokhi* introducing God's encounter with Israel
makes all human subjectivity, every human utterance
of *anokhi*, a reflection of the *anokhi* said by the One.
Put differently, for a human being to say "I am" is already a Divine revelation, and creates the potential for
deeper revelation.

By deepening the link between the Divine "I am"
and the human "I am" we create the fullness and the
promise of human life, the possibility of productivity
and creativity, the sweetness of sanctity, the aspiration
for justice and compassion. That link is the root meaning of Israel, and in its articulation in human action is
revealed the mystery of Israel's destiny.

In the modern democratic state of Israel, we have
become fearful of saying, "I am Israel." We are afraid
to say, "I am Israel" to ourselves, and most of all we
are afraid to say "I am Israel" to our children.

It is time to look in the mirror and to say, with conviction, "I am Israel." Revelation will surely follow.

THE BIRTH OF IRONY

Tisha Be'av

Gershom Gorenberg

At a party once, a friend with a receding hairline arrived with a guitar, sat on the floor in a back bedroom, and sang period-piece protest songs—the American "We Shall Overcome" and "we can change the world, rearrange the world," and the Israeli "Song of Peace." The melodies pulled people from other rooms and made them sit, sing, and close their eyes. My friend strummed with his eyes open, with an ironic half-smile. "What's funny?" I asked.

"You have to be a kid or a fool to believe this stuff, don't you?" he said. He wasn't singing songs of innocence, he was singing about them. And with another, unintentional irony, he had quoted an old script, about a far deeper loss of innocence. "From the time the Temple was destroyed," says the Talmud in Tractate *Bava Batra*, "prophecy was taken from prophets and given to fools and children."

A talmudic legend says the messiah was born the day the Temple fell. So was irony. Before the Destruction was pure joy and pure faith. "They say that he who never saw the celebration of the water libation [in the Temple on Sukkot] never saw celebration," the Mishnah tells us, and the words "they say" distance us. Joy like that was possible for them, because they didn't know destruction was coming.

Back then, real prophets spoke, or so people wholeheartedly believed. Now we half-smile at people who hear the Voice.

Dismissing prophecy was a practical matter. Tractate *Bava Metzia*, records a debate on laws of purity, in the generation after the Temple. Rabbi Elazar found his opinion rejected by the majority of sages.

> He said to them, "If the law is as I say, this carob tree will prove it." The carob tree moved a hundred cubits.
> They told him, "You can't bring evidence from a carob."
> He came back, "If the law is as I saw, the canal water will prove it." The water flowed backwards.
> They said to him, "You can't bring evidence from canal water." . . .
> He came back, "If the law is as I say, it will be proven from heaven." A voice came forth, saying, "What do you have against Rabbi Elazar, whose ruling is correct in every case?"
> Rabbi Yehoshua stood on his feet and said [quoting Deuteronomy 30:12], "It is not in heaven."

That debate established that Jewish law would be set, not by prophets, but by the majority of learned men. That was possible only after irony broke the force of wonders and charisma. Irony isn't disbelief. It's belief and disbelief together, hearing prophecy as such but also knowing that only a child could accept it without question. Quoting the revealed Bible, Rabbi Yehoshua declared that the age of revelation was over. Instead we have opinions, endless Jewish debate. The Mishnah, the Talmud—the great works of rabbinic argument—are post-Destruction. Irony, says one dictionary, is "a manner of organizing a work so as to give full expression to contradictory or complementary impulses, attitudes, etc." That sounds like a definition of Talmud.

Irony undermines passion. "We can change the world" becomes, with Woody Allen's intonation, "*We can change the world?*" You can read that as growing up or as growing old. Irony can keep you from following false prophets. It might also keep you from doing anything. So suggested Hebrew writer Haim Hazaz in his classic story, "The Sermon." A Zionist pioneer assaults all the generations that waited in Exile for the messiah: "Truly they believe with perfect faith . . . and yet, in the secrecy of their heart, you know, deep down, in some wrinkle, in some single hidden point in their heart, a little they don't believe . . . And that's also a Jewish trait, very very Jewish . . . a little bit not to believe, and to let that bit be decisive."

Problem is, it's harder to lose irony than to lose innocence, as hard as going backward to childhood. If sages suggested the Temple would be rebuilt only after the messiah came, perhaps it was because they knew how hard it would be to take prophecy back from fools—how hard to make cracked faith perfect again.

Come, let us mourn for the Temple.

CONTRIBUTORS

Susan Afterman is a poet and architect living in the Western Galilee. (*Vayakhel, Masei, Vezot Habrakhah*)

Mordechai Beck is a Jerusalem writer and printmaker who recently published a limited edition art book of Jonah with calligrapher David Moss. (*Pekudei*)

Jeremy Benstein is educational director of the Abraham Joshua Heschel Center for Nature Studies in Jerusalem. (*Yitro*)

S. Ben-Tov is completing her second book of poems. She is an assistant professor of creative writing at Ohio's Bowling Green State University. (Pesah—Seventh Day)

Rabbi Dov Berkovits teaches at Yakar and Elul, centers for Jewish education and culture in Jerusalem, and in Shilo, where he lives. (*Ki Tetze, Shavuot*)

Jonathan Blass is rabbi of the settlement of Neveh Tzuf and is the head of Ratzon Yehuda, a rabbinical seminary for graduates of *yeshivot hesder*. (*Aharei Mot.*)

Reuven P. Bulka is rabbi of Congregation Machzikei Hadas, Ottawa, Canada, and author of twenty-five books. (*Hahodesh*)

David Curzon is an Australian living in New York. He is the author of *Midrashim* (poems) and the editor of *"Modern Poems on the Bible: An Anthology"* and *"The Gospels in Our Image: An Anthology of Twentieth Century Poetry Based on Biblical Texts."* (*Hayyei Sarah, Metzora, Va'ethanan*)

Dr. Zeev Dashevsky is an astrophysicist who headed a pre-perestroika Jewish learning group in Moscow. After thirteen years as a refusenik, he arrived in Jerusalem on Holocaust Day, 1990. He heads Machanaim, a Jewish heritage center for Jews from the former Soviet Union.(Counting of the Omer)

Dr. Seymour Epstein, based in Jerusalem, is director of Jewish education at the American Jewish Joint Distribution Committee. (Purim)

Dr. Baruch Feldstern is a director of academic affairs at Pardes Institute of Jewish Studies in Jerusalem. (*Toldot*)

Everett Fox is associate professor of Judaica and director of Jewish Studies at Clark University in Massachusetts. His *The Five Books of Moses, A New Translation, with Introductions, Commentary and Notes* was recently published by Schocken Books. (*Vayikra*)

Menahem Froman is rabbi of Teko'a and is active in interreligious dialogue between Jewish settlers and Palestinian Muslims. (*Shkalim*)

Rabbi Pinchas Giller, a professor of Jewish studies at Washington University in St. Louis, is the author of *The Enlightened Will Shine: Symbolization and Theurgy in the Later Strata of the Zohar.* (*Ha'azinu*)

Gershom Gorenberg is the opinion editor of *The Jerusalem Report.* (*Miketz, Pinhas, Zakhor,* Yom Kippur, Sukkot— Intermediary Sabbath, Pesah, Tisha Be'av)

Blu Greenberg is the author of *On Women and Judaism* and *How to Run a Traditional Jewish Household.* (*Dvarim, Shoftim*)

Rabbi Irving Greenberg is president of CLAL, the National Jewish Center for Learning and Leadership in New York, and author of *The Jewish Way.* (*Breshit, Va'era*)

Ed Greenstein, professor of Bible at the Jewish Theological Seminary, is co-author of *The Timetables of Jewish History.* (*Trumah*)

Dr. Bonna Devora Haberman is a philosopher, Jewish educator, and social activist committed to Torah and exegesis using tools of feminist scholarship. (*Vayishlah*)

Hillel Halkin is a literary critic, translator of Hebrew and Yiddish literature, staff writer for the *Forward* weekly, and author of *Letters to an American Jewish Friend: A Zionist's Polemic*. (*Beshallah, Shlah Lekha, Balak*)

Professor Reuven Hammer of the Masorti Movement's Seminary of Judaic Studies and the Hebrew University is the author of *Entering Jewish Prayer* and *The Classic Midrash*. His most recent work, *The Jerusalem Anthology: A Literary Guide* was published by JPS. (*Hukkat, Matot*)

Shulamith Hareven is a Jerusalem novelist. Her biblical trilogy, *The Miracle Hater, Prophet*, and *After Childhood*, relates to the transition to monotheism. She describes herself as agnostic, and sees her Judaism in terms of continued study of the sources and the duty to create new midrash. (*Behukkotai*)

Barry W. Holtz is associate professor of Jewish education at the Jewish Theological Seminary of America. (*Nitzavim*)

Bethamie Horowitz is director of planning and research at UJA-Federation of New York. (*Nitzavim*)

Paula Hyman is the Lucy Moses Professor of Modern Jewish History at Yale University. Her most recent book is *Gender and Assimilation in Modern Jewish History*. (Sukkot)

Lord Jakobovits is the former chief rabbi of Britain and the Commonwealth. (*Noah*)

Rabbi Daniel Landes is director of Pardes Institute of Jewish Studies in Jerusalem. (*Vayera*, Pesah—Intermediary Sabbath)

Yeshayahu Leibowitz was head of the biological chemistry department at the Hebrew University and professor of neurophysiology at the university's medical school; after his retirement in 1973, he was a lecturer in the philosophy department. He was also editor-in-chief of the Hebrew Encyclopedia. (*Vayetze, Shmini, Beha'alotkha, Korah, Re'eh*)

Rabbi Tzvi Marx is director of applied education at the Shalom Hartman Institute and author of *Halakha and*

Handicap: Jewish Law and Ethics on Disability. (*Tazria, Ki Tavo*)

Rabbi Micha Odenheimer is a Jerusalem journalist and teacher, and is the director of the Israel Association for Ethiopian Jews. (*Kedoshim, Bemidbar, Naso, Vayelekh, Hanukkah*)

Rabbi W. Gunther Plaut, senior scholar of Holy Blossom Temple in Toronto, is a biblical scholar and historian. He is the editor and principal author of *The Torah—a Modern Commentary*, published by UAHC, and author of a new commentary on the *haftarot*. (*Vayehi, Tzav*)

Rabbi Nachum L. Rabinovitch heads the *hesder* yeshivah in Ma'aleh Adumim. He is the author of a comprehensive commentary on Maimonides' Code. His other works include a history of probability and statistics. (*Mishpatim*)

Nessa Rapoport is the author of a novel, *Preparing for Sabbath*, and of *A Woman's Book of Grieving*. With Ted Solotaroff, she edited *Writing Our Way Home: Contemporary Stories by American Jewish Writers*. (*Emor*)

David Rosen, former chief rabbi of Ireland, is director of interfaith relations for the Anti-Defamation League's Israel office and its liaison to the Vatican, and is president of the World Conference on Religion and Peace. (*Ki Tissa*)

Michael Rosenak is Mandel Professor of Jewish Education at the Melton Center for Jewish Education at the Hebrew University. His most recent book is *Roads to the Palace: Jewish Texts and Teaching*. (*Tetzaveh*)

Stuart Schoffman is a columnist and critic for *The Jerusalem Report*, and the screenwriter of *The Wordmaker*, a drama about Eliezer Ben- Yehuda. (*Lekh Lekha*)

Rabbi Harold M. Schulweis is spiritual leader of Valley Beth Shalom in Encino, California, founding chairman of the Jewish Foundation for Christian Rescuers, and author of *For Those Who Can't Believe: Overcoming the Obstacles to Faith*. (*Behar*)

Dr. Baruch J. Schwartz is a lecturer in Bible at Tel Aviv University. His area of interest is biblical law and cultic institutions. (*Parah*)

Professor Avigdor Shinan teaches midrashic literature at the Hebrew University. (*Vayigash*)

Dr. Marc Silverman teaches at the Melton Center of Jewish Education at the Hebrew University, and is writing a book on the contemporary significance of Zionism and Israel. (*Ekev*)

Fredelle Z. Spiegel is a member of the Jewish Studies Faculty at UCLA, research clinical associate of the Southern California Psychoanalytic Institute, and author of *Women's Wages, Women's Worth: Politics, Religion, and Equity.* (*Bo*)

Rabbi Moshe David Tendler is professor of talmudic law and medical ethics and chairman of the biology department at Yeshiva University. (Rosh Hashanah)

Dr. Deborah Weissman is director of the Kerem Institute for Humanistic Jewish Education in Jerusalem. (*Shmot*)

Rabbi Moshe Zemer directs the Institute of Progressive Halakhah and is head of the rabbinic court of the Israel Council of Progressive Rabbis. (*Vayeshev*)

INDEX

About the Editor

Gershom Gorenberg is the opinion editor and a columnist at The Jerusalem Report, a regular contributor to The New Republic, and a co-author of Shalom, Friend: The Life and Legacy of Yitzhak Rabin (Newmarket Press, 1995). As a journalist, he has written extensively on Jewish religious issues, and his poetry has appeared in literary journals in the U.S. and England. Gorenberg has an M.A. in Jewish education from The Hebrew University. He moved to Israel from California in 1977 and lives in Jerusalem with his wife, Myra Noveck, and their three children.